Optimum Life Journal

Live your Optimum Life through gratitude
and conscious achievement.

This journal belongs to:

....

From: /   / 20   To: /   / 20

Helene Kempe & David Nolan

OptimumThinking.net

Copyright © 2013 by Optimum Thinking. All rights reserved except as permitted under the Australian Copyright Act of 1968. No part of this publication may be reproduced or distributed in any form or by any means, or stored in a data base retrieval system, without prior written permission of the authors.

ISBN: 978-0-9924465-1-2

ACKNOWLEDGEMENTS

We would like to acknowledge that this journal has been inspired by ideas from the many personal development leaders whose work we have studied.

Graphic design and layout by Kimberly Cook and Kierrah Jill M. Tanglao

Contents

Introduction	5
Optimum Life Scope	7
Optimum Life Masterpiece	10
Daily Journal Instructions	14
Gratitude	15
Daily Flip It	16
Conscious Intention and Priorities	17
Annual Calendar	18
12 Month Intention Plan	20
Monthly Intention Plan—January	22
Monthly Intention Plan—February	56
Monthly Intention Plan—March	88
Monthly Intention Plan—April	122
Monthly Intention Plan—May	154
Monthly Intention Plan—June	188
Monthly Intention Plan—July	220
Monthly Intention Plan—August	254
Monthly Intention Plan—September	288
Monthly Intention Plan—October	320
Monthly Intention Plan—November	354
Monthly Intention Plan—December	386
A Work in Progress	419

Through the challenge of transformation, the butterfly gains the strength and direction to fly.

Introduction

This journal has been designed to help you consciously create the life that you really want. The clearer you are about what you want, the more easily you will create it. The frustration you feel about what you haven't yet achieved is always directly in proportion to the lack of detail you include in your planning.

There is only one person who gets up in the morning and dedicates their life to living your best life — make everyday count!

The journal provides you the structure to plan at a high level annually, monthly and daily. It is easy to follow and once you make it a habit to use your journal daily, you will start to see amazing progress towards your Highest Individual Life Priorities (HILP). As you become more aware daily of what you value and how you spend your resources of time, money, energy and thought, you will be able to direct your focus on what you most want to achieve. When you leave time unplanned, it is quickly filled with other people's priorities. The more you consciously choose how to use your resources to achieve your highest priorities, the more fulfilled your life becomes. Once you complete your planning at this higher level, transfer your Life Priorities to your daily planning.

To make the most of this journal follow these simple steps:

1. Read the introduction and instructions for each section.

2. Then schedule time to complete your:
   ☐ Optimum Life Scope
   ☐ Optimum Life Masterpiece
   ☐ 12 Month Intention Plan

3. Put dates in the Annual Calendar for all of the important events in the year to come.

4. Then schedule some time to do your first Monthly Intention Plan. At the end of each month, review your goals before writing the ones for the coming month. This is a very valuable process to help you set realistic goals.

5. At the end of each day allocate time in your evening routine to complete the Daily Gratitude and Intention page — you only need 10 mins a day to practise your Optimum Thinking skills and accelerate the creation of your Optimum Life!

Listen to your heart and ask yourself what you would really **love to be, to do and to have** in your life.

Optimum Life Scope

To empower your life it is essential to get clear on what is really important for **you** to have and achieve in your life. When you think of the things you are going to do in a day, if you hear yourself saying "I have to do...." or "I must do...." or "I should...." then you are living parts of your life according to what you think other people want you to do. Listen to your heart and ask yourself what you would really **love to be, to do and to have** in your life. Take some time to sit down and reflect on what really inspires you, what you want to achieve in this life and what difference you would like to make or service you would like to provide for others. It's impossible to put a wrong answer — they are yours and only you truly know what you want to dedicate your life to. Don't say "I don't know." — You are the only one who definitely does know. So, if you have never done this before, just start...make this your first draft — you have the power to change it whenever you like!

Once you get clear on what you really want in your life, these Life Priorities become your compass you can check in with every time an opportunity comes your way or there is a decision to make.

Reviewing your Life Priorities regularly (quarterly at least) helps ensure you are conscious of what you are doing with your life — after all you only get one go to live your life in your current body, so why not make sure you do as much of what you love as possible. We all leave a legacy when we leave the planet — why not leave a legacy you create on purpose rather than by accident?

To assist you to empower all areas of your life, your Optimum Life Scope is divided into 7 areas: Spiritual, Mental/Education, Vocational/Career, Financial/Saving/Investing, Familial/Relationship, Social/Friends/Networks and Health & Physical Apprearance.

Make sure you take the time to put something down for every area of your life. If there is an area you choose to ignore, you can be sure someone else will start running your life in that area. In fact other people can only overpower you if you choose to stay under educated and don't take action in an area. It is wise to ensure you pay enough attention to all areas of your life in which you would like to have fulfilment.

Now, go to a quiet place where you won't get interrupted, get comfortable, get focussed and write out your top Life Priorities in each of the areas of life.

Optimum Life Scope

Use conscious intention and write a description of your Optimum Life...

SPIRITUAL / MISSION / SELF-ACTUALIZATION

....
....
....
....
....
....
....
....

MENTAL / EDUCATION

....
....
....
....
....
....
....
....

VOCATION / CAREER

....
....
....
....
....
....
....
....

FINANCIAL WEALTH / SAVING & INVESTING

....
....
....
....
....
....
....

FAMILY / RELATIONSHIP

....
....
....
....
....
....
....

SOCIAL / FRIENDS / NETWORKS

....
....
....
....
....
....
....

HEALTH & PHYSICAL APPEARANCE

....
....
....
....
....
....
....

Optimum Life Masterpiece

Compose a visual masterpiece for your Optimum Life. Collages of images help your sub-conscious mind focus on what you want to create in your life. We remember everything as images, even words...how many times have you had to write a tricky word down so you could see what it looks like before you knew you had the spelling accurate? By creating a collage of images you give your subconscious mind high quality data and clarity about what you want to focus on achieving in your life.

Your subconscious mind is incredibly powerful and is running your mind and body more than 95% of the time so it is really, really, **really** important to let it know what you want to achieve in as much detail as you can!

The first step is to collect or draw images to use. If you can't find a picture of what you want in magazines, search the internet and print them out. Flick though images and notice when you see things that create an inspired response in your heart — the stronger you feel inspired by the image, the more likely it is that it will be part of your future. The inspiration may be that you want to do the same as is in the image, or it may be that the image provokes in you the desire to make a positive difference in some way.

Drawing the images is also really powerful as your physical body is even more engaged in the creative process. Don't get hung up on the quality of your drawings or who might see them; you only need to represent the images you see in your mind with as much detail as you need to bring the full image back to mind. Play with colour in your drawings and for decorating your masterpiece. The more vividly you create your Optimum Life Masterpiece, the more easily you will hold it in mind.

Most importantly — have fun creating!

You are the only person who knows what you want — this is all about consciously creating an inspirational life for yourself. Look for the images of what you are prepared to work hard to bring into your life. Things that you are prepared to work through challenges to achieve — as humans we are wired with a desire to "play a bigger game" and we do that through overcoming challenges.

As in everything in life, you get back what you put in. If you only collect a whole lot of images of "stuff" that society projects as "the good life" and glue them in, you may fail to bring them into your life. It is fine to have nice "things" just ensure you also include images about your life purpose. To have your Optimum Life Masterpiece come to fruition, it is really important that you tune in at both a conscious and spiritual level to ensure you are including things that truly inspire you.

Your soul will never be fulfilled through acquiring physical things.

When you include images that appeal to your authentic self you unleash the power of your imagination. Focus and quieten yourself then reflect on each image. Ask yourself what achieving or obtaining each thing will really mean to you. If it is important and you get a tear of inspiration, add it. If it feels superficial and just about "keeping up with the Jones'" let it go. Once you filter the images and connect with how they will help you fulfil your life purpose, your unconscious mind will automatically start asking incredibly creative and powerful questions that will help you move towards what you have included. Combinations of what you have included will start to stick in your mind and steer you towards making the vision real.

Ensure your Optimum Life Masterpiece includes images of things that are worth devoting your life to — because every day you get up and live, **you are always investing your life** in what you choose to spend your time doing!

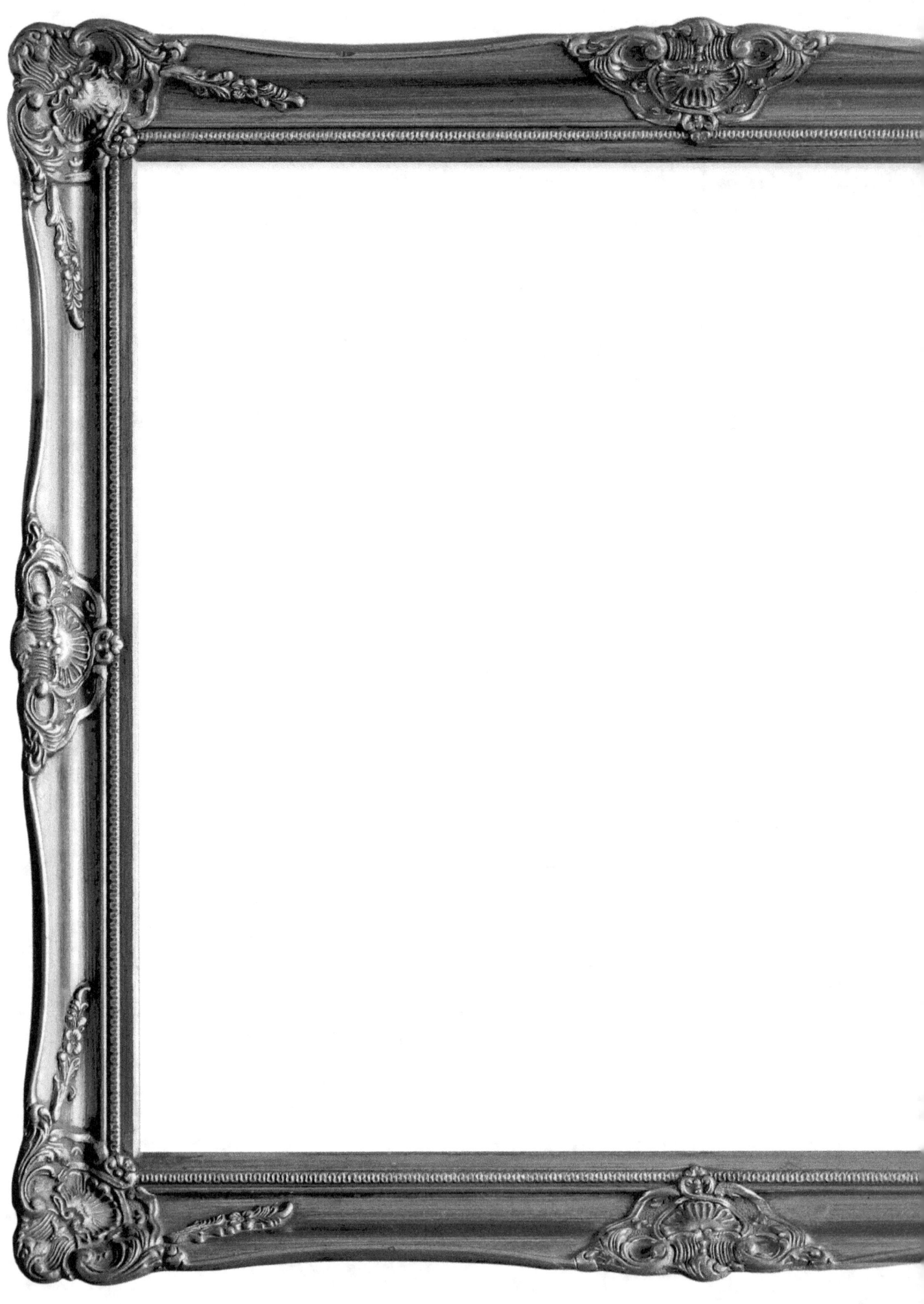

Daily Journal Instructions

The individual day pages of this journal include either a quote about gratitude or a reminder for developing your Optimum Thinking skills and mindset. Take a few moments each day to read and reflect on them.

Then fill in the three key areas each day: gratitude, your daily challenge to practise your Optimum Thinking and your highest priorities for the following day.

Gratitude

The power of gratitude should never be underestimated. Taking some time to reflect and be grateful for your life creates amazing shifts in perception that help you lead a fulfilling and empowered life.

Whenever you feel gratitude, scientists have proven that your brain 'rewards' you by releasing dopamine and serotonin that are our inbuilt "feel-good" drugs. We are also rewarded with feeling more inspired. As Dr Antonio Damasio, a neuroscientist is quoted as saying "We are not thinking machines that feel, but emotional machines that think."

Some people wish they were given all they want in life. In reality however, if we were only ever supported and given all that we ask for; life would soon become very boring and we would have no reason to grow or achieve.

When we start to look for, and really appreciate the benefits we receive from the challenges we face in our lives, we truly start to expand our perception of what is possible to achieve in our life. Our greatest growth occurs when there is a little chaos from challenge balanced by just enough support to keep us stable.

At the end of each day, take a few minutes to reflect on what you are truly grateful for in your life. Make a list of people, things and entities that assisted you that day so you can appreciate all of the ways you are supported by others. Also make sure you thank yourself for who you have served and what you have achieved each day. To maintain your peception of living your optimum and fulfilled life is important to keep a balanced perception of service-to-self being equal to service-to-others. Reflect on your list and take a few moments to feel the appreciation in your heart — when you are truly grateful, you will create a tear of inspiration in your eye.

If you are ever feeling low and having a self pity party, write a list of every person and thing for which you are grateful. Keep going until you feel your energy shift back to the point where you can again appreciate what an amazing opportunity life offers you to connect, learn and achieve. Start with the small things and work up from there. You will find them once you search in all areas of your life. Also write down how the things you are grateful for will help you achieve your Life Priorities.

Daily Flip It

Next look for what your biggest challenge was in the day and find all of the ways that challenge will also assist you to achieve your Life Priorities. At first you may think there is no possible way a particular challenge helped you; look again and again. Think about how the challenge: taught you something; gave you a chance to practice a new skill; improved your character and/or strengthened your determination. Consider how the lesson learned or skill practised will help you in each of the areas of your life as you move forward. What will it help you achieve? What will it help you avoid that might cost you dearly in the future? For example if someone shouted at you and you felt hurt, it might mean you have practised resiliance and that you decide to improve how you communicate with that person. The next step is to ask yourself how improving your communication will be a benefit to you in all areas of your life. Who else will you be able to communicate more clearly with and how will that help you get what you want in life.

Keep finding benefits you received from each challenge until you are certain there was equal benefits as drawbacks and you will be able to shift your perception of the event to a level of true appreciation and gratitude for the amazing universe in which we live. This reduces fear of it happening again and empowers you to move forward with achieving what you want.

We all understand that when we perceive something as being negative that we want to get rid of the negative feeling in our system. However, there is an equally powerful daily challenge you can balance when you are infatuated with something that happened that you think is really wonderful. When we stay infatuated with something (or someone) it means we are only seeing one side of the situation. This "half blindness" makes us vulnerable and means people are able to take advantage of us. When we keep replaying a fantasy in our mind, we create endorphines that make us feel good – the problem with this is that the endorphines are addictive and we can get stuck trying to live in the fantasy and therefore become ungrateful for our life as it really is.

To bring an infatuation back to balance, we need to ask ourself how the perceived "wonderful" event is actually a drawback to us; how it will hold us back in other areas of our life and/or what it will cost us to have this "wonderful" thing or person in our lives.

In both cases, we are working to bring our perception back to a balance where we can see that **every action / inaction has both sides equally**. When we are seeing only one side, we are in emotional reaction. When we see both sides equally, we are able to get back into inspired action.

Conscious Intention and Priorities

To complete the final section each evening, take a few moments to write out your top 5 to 7 highest priority action steps for the following day that will move you towards achieving your long-term goals. In the evening is the best time to set your priorities for the next day as it allows your subconscious mind to process it for you throughout the night and gain additional clarity before you take action the following day. Remember if you don't set your priorities for your day, someone else will.

Nobody likes to be told what to do. When you consciously take control of where you invest your resources you feel more in contol of your life.

Time is your most precious resource — once you have used it, you can never get it back! The more consciously you set your priorities for activities you do, the easier it will be for you to achieve your Highest Individual Life Priorities (HILP).

The more frequently you use your Executive (Higher) Mind to direct your Animal (Lower) Mind them more you will be able to consiously achieve what you want in life.

It takes work and consistent repetition to devleop new empowering habits. You have to train yourelf to use your Executive Mind to direct your actions, as your Animal Mind is the part of you that lives in the delusion you can have pleasure without pain and tries to avoid overcoming the challenges it takes to live a fulfilling life where you make a meaningful difference to others and yourself.

When you set your highest priorities daily and take action on them, you achieve more of what you want in your life. Once you make this a habit, you will discover that it is such a powerful thing to do that you will wonder why you didn't start doing it sooner.

In this busy world ... remember to prioritize your priorities!

Annual Calendar

January	February	March	April	May	June
1	1	1	1	1	1
2	2	2	2	2	2
3	3	3	3	3	3
4	4	4	4	4	4
5	5	5	5	5	5
6	6	6	6	6	6
7	7	7	7	7	7
8	8	8	8	8	8
9	9	9	9	9	9
10	10	10	10	10	10
11	11	11	11	11	11
12	12	12	12	12	12
13	13	13	13	13	13
14	14	14	14	14	14
15	15	15	15	15	15
16	16	16	16	16	16
17	17	17	17	17	17
18	18	18	18	18	18
19	19	19	19	19	19
20	20	20	20	20	20
21	21	21	21	21	21
22	22	22	22	22	22
23	23	23	23	23	23
24	24	24	24	24	24
25	25	25	25	25	25
26	26	26	26	26	26
27	27	27	27	27	27
28	28	28	28	28	28
29	29	29	29	29	29
30		30	30	30	30
31		31		31	

July	August	September	October	November	December
1	1	1	1	1	1
2	2	2	2	2	2
3	3	3	3	3	3
4	4	4	4	4	4
5	5	5	5	5	5
6	6	6	6	6	6
7	7	7	7	7	7
8	8	8	8	8	8
9	9	9	9	9	9
10	10	10	10	10	10
11	11	11	11	11	11
12	12	12	12	12	12
13	13	13	13	13	13
14	14	14	14	14	14
15	15	15	15	15	15
16	16	16	16	16	16
17	17	17	17	17	17
18	18	18	18	18	18
19	19	19	19	19	19
20	20	20	20	20	20
21	21	21	21	21	21
22	22	22	22	22	22
23	23	23	23	23	23
24	24	24	24	24	24
25	25	25	25	25	25
26	26	26	26	26	26
27	27	27	27	27	27
28	28	28	28	28	28
29	29	29	29	29	29
30	30	30	30	30	30
31	31		31		31

12 Month Intention Plan

Another way to set powerful intentions for your life is to write a word story of this day one year from now as you intend to create it. Be specific and add details about every area of your life. Read it aloud to yourself and if possible to another person and notice how it feels when you reflect on what you have achieved in your life.

It is now .... and I am so grateful that ....
(One year later – same date and month)

JANUARY

Monthly Intention Plan

Write the top priorities you intend to focus on in each area of your life during this month.

SPIRITUAL / MISSION / SELF-ACTUALIZATION

MENTAL / EDUCATION

VOCATION / CAREER

FINANCIAL WEALTH / SAVING & INVESTING

FAMILY / RELATIONSHIP

SOCIAL / FRIENDS

HEALTH & PHYSICAL APPEARANCE

JAN 1

You think me a child of circumstances. I make my circumstances.
— Ralph Waldo Emerson

Daily Gratitude and Intention

Today I am grateful for:
- Balance perception of service to self = service to others
- Look in all areas of life

Today's Flip It:
- Balance perceived negative action/inaction until benefits = drawbacks
- Balance perceived positive action/inaction until drawbacks = benefits

My highest priority actions for tomorrow:

There is always the exact opposite positive in any perceived negative behaviour occuring at the exact same moment. Practice finding it in little moments and it will help you balance the bigger challenges faster. — Optimum Thinking

JAN 2

Daily Gratitude and Intention

Today I am grateful for:
- Balance perception of service to self = service to others
- Look in all areas of life

Today's Flip It:
- Balance perceived negative action/inaction until benefits = drawbacks
- Balance perceived positive action/inaction until drawbacks = benefits

My highest priority actions for tomorrow:

JAN 3

A grateful mind is a great mind which eventually attracts to itself great things. — Plato

Daily Gratitude and Intention

Today I am grateful for:
- Balance perception of service to self = service to others
- Look in all areas of life

Today's Flip It:
- Balance perceived negative action/inaction until benefits = drawbacks
- Balance perceived positive action/inaction until drawbacks = benefits

My highest priority actions for tomorrow:

No one can make you feel anything. Owning and understanding this is fundamental to mastering your emotions. — Optimum Thinking

JAN 4

Daily Gratitude and Intention

Today I am grateful for:
- Balance perception of service to self = service to others
- Look in all areas of life

Today's Flip It:
- Balance perceived negative action/inaction until benefits = drawbacks
- Balance perceived positive action/inaction until drawbacks = benefits

My highest priority actions for tomorrow:

JAN 5

Gratitude does not seek endebtedness. Gratitude appreciates that there is always fair exchange. — Optimum Thinking

Daily Gratitude and Intention

Today I am grateful for:
- Balance perception of service to self = service to others
- Look in all areas of life

Today's Flip It:
- Balance perceived negative action/inaction until benefits = drawbacks
- Balance perceived positive action/inaction until drawbacks = benefits

My highest priority actions for tomorrow:

We are all Meaning Making Machines. We create our emotions with the meanings we make about what we perceive to have happened.
— Optimum Thinking

JAN 6

Daily Gratitude and Intention

Today I am grateful for:
- Balance perception of service to self = service to others
- Look in all areas of life

Today's Flip It:
- Balance perceived negative action/inaction until benefits = drawbacks
- Balance perceived positive action/inaction until drawbacks = benefits

My highest priority actions for tomorrow:

JAN 7

A grateful mindset can set you free from the prison of disempowerment and the shackles of misery. — Steve Maraboli

Daily Gratitude and Intention

Today I am grateful for:
- Balance perception of service to self = service to others
- Look in all areas of life

Today's Flip It:
- Balance perceived negative action/inaction until benefits = drawbacks
- Balance perceived positive action/inaction until drawbacks = benefits

My highest priority actions for tomorrow:

Every action or inaction we choose is a strategy to get what we want. — Optimum Thinking

JAN 8

Daily Gratitude and Intention

Today I am grateful for:
- Balance perception of service to self = service to others
- Look in all areas of life

Today's Flip It:
- Balance perceived negative action/inaction until benefits = drawbacks
- Balance perceived positive action/inaction until drawbacks = benefits

My highest priority actions for tomorrow:

JAN 9

Acknowledging the good that you already have in your life is the foundation for all abundance. — Eckhart Tolle

Daily Gratitude and Intention

Today I am grateful for:
- Balance perception of service to self = service to others
- Look in all areas of life

Today's Flip It:
- Balance perceived negative action/inaction until benefits = drawbacks
- Balance perceived positive action/inaction until drawbacks = benefits

My highest priority actions for tomorrow:

Research has shown that we distort our memories by up to 50% based on how we filter an event. We all believe we are more right than other people when we recall an event ... that is why often agreeing on what actually happened can be a slippery eel to catch. — Optimum Thinking

JAN 10

Daily Gratitude and Intention

Today I am grateful for:
- Balance perception of service to self = service to others
- Look in all areas of life

Today's Flip It:
- Balance perceived negative action/inaction until benefits = drawbacks
- Balance perceived positive action/inaction until drawbacks = benefits

My highest priority actions for tomorrow:

JAN 11

Gratitude for yourself and for those who have helped you is reflection on the past and assures you support will come as you continue to challenge yourself to grow and play a bigger game!
— Optimum Thinking

Daily Gratitude and Intention

Today I am grateful for:
- Balance perception of service to self = service to others
- Look in all areas of life

Today's Flip It:
- Balance perceived negative action/inaction until benefits = drawbacks
- Balance perceived positive action/inaction until drawbacks = benefits

My highest priority actions for tomorrow:

> There is no such thing as "good" people and "bad" people. It is more empowering to see everyone as an "Agent of the Universe" with a hierarchy of individual life priorities (HILP) trying to get what they want. — *Optimum Thinking*

JAN 12

Daily Gratitude and Intention

Today I am grateful for:
- Balance perception of service to self = service to others
- Look in all areas of life

....

Today's Flip It:
- Balance perceived negative action/inaction until benefits = drawbacks
- Balance perceived positive action/inaction until drawbacks = benefits

....

My highest priority actions for tomorrow:

....

JAN 13

All that we behold is full of blessings.
— William Wordsworth

Daily Gratitude and Intention

Today I am grateful for:
- Balance perception of service to self = service to others
- Look in all areas of life

Today's Flip It:
- Balance perceived negative action/inaction until benefits = drawbacks
- Balance perceived positive action/inaction until drawbacks = benefits

My highest priority actions for tomorrow:

We all possess every action and inaction we list on our polarized "good person" and "bad person" list and we choose to use whatever we believe will get us the best result in the moment. — Optimum Thinking

JAN 14

Daily Gratitude and Intention

Today I am grateful for:
- Balance perception of service to self = service to others
- Look in all areas of life

Today's Flip It:
- Balance perceived negative action/inaction until benefits = drawbacks
- Balance perceived positive action/inaction until drawbacks = benefits

My highest priority actions for tomorrow:

JAN 15

Appreciation can make a day, even change a life. Your willingness to put it into words is all that is necessary.
— Margaret Cousins

Daily Gratitude and Intention

Today I am grateful for:
- Balance perception of service to self = service to others
- Look in all areas of life

Today's Flip It:
- Balance perceived negative action/inaction until benefits = drawbacks
- Balance perceived positive action/inaction until drawbacks = benefits

My highest priority actions for tomorrow:

Overdogs attract humbling circumstances. If you feel yourself puffing up and getting proud, ask yourself the right questions to bring you back to balance before external forces do. — Optimum Thinking

JAN 16

Daily Gratitude and Intention

Today I am grateful for:
- Balance perception of service to self = service to others
- Look in all areas of life

Today's Flip It:
- Balance perceived negative action/inaction until benefits = drawbacks
- Balance perceived positive action/inaction until drawbacks = benefits

My highest priority actions for tomorrow:

JAN 17

If you ever wake up without a problem, you better get on your hands and knees and pray for one; for otherwise you have died. — Norman Vincent Peale (author - The Power of Positive Thinking)

Daily Gratitude and Intention

Today I am grateful for:
- Balance perception of service to self = service to others
- Look in all areas of life

Today's Flip It:
- Balance perceived negative action/inaction until benefits = drawbacks
- Balance perceived positive action/inaction until drawbacks = benefits

My highest priority actions for tomorrow:

We each use whatever action or inaction we believe will give us the most benefit at the time...so does everyone else.
— Optimum Thinking

JAN 18

Daily Gratitude and Intention

Today I am grateful for:
- Balance perception of service to self = service to others
- Look in all areas of life

Today's Flip It:
- Balance perceived negative action/inaction until benefits = drawbacks
- Balance perceived positive action/inaction until drawbacks = benefits

My highest priority actions for tomorrow:

JAN 19

Nothing would mean anything if I didn't live a life of use to others. — Anjelina Jolie

Daily Gratitude and Intention

Today I am grateful for:
- Balance perception of service to self = service to others
- Look in all areas of life

Today's Flip It:
- Balance perceived negative action/inaction until benefits = drawbacks
- Balance perceived positive action/inaction until drawbacks = benefits

My highest priority actions for tomorrow:

Gratitude is the most attractive vibrational frequency. You can't fake it; you have to do the work to open your heart. — Optimum Thinking

JAN 20

Daily Gratitude and Intention

Today I am grateful for:
- Balance perception of service to self = service to others
- Look in all areas of life

Today's Flip It:
- Balance perceived negative action/inaction until benefits = drawbacks
- Balance perceived positive action/inaction until drawbacks = benefits

My highest priority actions for tomorrow:

JAN 21

As each day comes to us refreshed and anew, so does my gratitude renews itself daily. The breaking of the sun over the horizon is my grateful heart dawning upon a blessed world. — Terri Guillemets

Daily Gratitude and Intention

Today I am grateful for:
- Balance perception of service to self = service to others
- Look in all areas of life

Today's Flip It:
- Balance perceived negative action/inaction until benefits = drawbacks
- Balance perceived positive action/inaction until drawbacks = benefits

My highest priority actions for tomorrow:

Practice your Optimum Thinking daily and harness the power of positive and negative thinking. — Optimum Thinking

JAN 22

Daily Gratitude and Intention

Today I am grateful for:
- Balance perception of service to self = service to others
- Look in all areas of life

Today's Flip It:
- Balance perceived negative action/inaction until benefits = drawbacks
- Balance perceived positive action/inaction until drawbacks = benefits

My highest priority actions for tomorrow:

JAN 23

As we express our gratitude, we must never forget that the highest appreciation is not to utter words, but to live by them.
— John Fitzgerald Kennedy

Daily Gratitude and Intention

Today I am grateful for:
- Balance perception of service to self = service to others
- Look in all areas of life

Today's Flip It:
- Balance perceived negative action/inaction until benefits = drawbacks
- Balance perceived positive action/inaction until drawbacks = benefits

My highest priority actions for tomorrow:

Optimum Dogs are humbly empowered, know what they want and are prepared to embrace both support and challenge to achieve their mission. — *Optimum Thinking*

JAN 24

Daily Gratitude and Intention

Today I am grateful for:
- Balance perception of service to self = service to others
- Look in all areas of life

Today's Flip It:
- Balance perceived negative action/inaction until benefits = drawbacks
- Balance perceived positive action/inaction until drawbacks = benefits

My highest priority actions for tomorrow:

JAN 25

He who knows enough is enough, will always have enough.
— Lao Tzu

Daily Gratitude and Intention

Today I am grateful for:
- Balance perception of service to self = service to others
- Look in all areas of life

Today's Flip It:
- Balance perceived negative action/inaction until benefits = drawbacks
- Balance perceived positive action/inaction until drawbacks = benefits

My highest priority actions for tomorrow:

Competitors compete with each other. Champions compete with themselves. — Optimum Thinking

JAN 26

Daily Gratitude and Intention

Today I am grateful for:
- Balance perception of service to self = service to others
- Look in all areas of life

Today's Flip It:
- Balance perceived negative action/inaction until benefits = drawbacks
- Balance perceived positive action/inaction until drawbacks = benefits

My highest priority actions for tomorrow:

JAN 27

Be grateful for the tiny details of your life and make room for unexpected and beautiful blessings. — Anonymous

Daily Gratitude and Intention

Today I am grateful for:
- Balance perception of service to self = service to others
- Look in all areas of life

Today's Flip It:
- Balance perceived negative action/inaction until benefits = drawbacks
- Balance perceived positive action/inaction until drawbacks = benefits

My highest priority actions for tomorrow:

If you are doing a 'pity party' take the time to list what you are grateful for in all areas of your life. Keep this list, re-read it and add to it any time in the future you find yourself slipping into a negative state. There is always fair exchange.
— Optimum Thinking

JAN 28

Daily Gratitude and Intention

Today I am grateful for:
- Balance perception of service to self = service to others
- Look in all areas of life

Today's Flip It:
- Balance perceived negative action/inaction until benefits = drawbacks
- Balance perceived positive action/inaction until drawbacks = benefits

My highest priority actions for tomorrow:

JAN 29

Be content with what you have; rejoice in the way things are. When you realize there is nothing lacking, the whole world belongs to you. — Lao Tzu

Daily Gratitude and Intention

Today I am grateful for:
- Balance perception of service to self = service to others
- Look in all areas of life

Today's Flip It:
- Balance perceived negative action/inaction until benefits = drawbacks
- Balance perceived positive action/inaction until drawbacks = benefits

My highest priority actions for tomorrow:

Infatuation keeps us stuck in fantasy and reduces our ability to live in and appreciate the present and the gifts life has already given us. — Optimum Thinking

JAN 30

Daily Gratitude and Intention

Today I am grateful for:
- Balance perception of service to self = service to others
- Look in all areas of life

Today's Flip It:
- Balance perceived negative action/inaction until benefits = drawbacks
- Balance perceived positive action/inaction until drawbacks = benefits

My highest priority actions for tomorrow:

JAN 31

It is good to have an end to journey toward, but it is the journey that matters in the end. — Ursula K. Leguin

Daily Gratitude and Intention

Today I am grateful for:
- Balance perception of service to self = service to others
- Look in all areas of life

Today's Flip It:
- Balance perceived negative action/inaction until benefits = drawbacks
- Balance perceived positive action/inaction until drawbacks = benefits

My highest priority actions for tomorrow:

FEBRUARY

Monthly Intention Plan

Write the top priorities you intend to focus on in each area of your life during this month.

SPIRITUAL / MISSION / SELF-ACTUALIZATION

MENTAL / EDUCATION

VOCATION / CAREER

FINANCIAL WEALTH / SAVING & INVESTING

FAMILY / RELATIONSHIP

SOCIAL / FRIENDS

HEALTH & PHYSICAL APPEARANCE

FEB 1

The deepest craving of human nature is the need to be appreciated. — William James

Daily Gratitude and Intention

Today I am grateful for:
- Balance perception of service to self = service to others
- Look in all areas of life

Today's Flip It:
- Balance perceived negative action/inaction until benefits = drawbacks
- Balance perceived positive action/inaction until drawbacks = benefits

My highest priority actions for tomorrow:

The only constant is transformation. Take the time to find equal benefits and drawbacks in any transformation you perceive in your life as they occur. This will help you stay balanced, grateful and vital. — Optimum Thinking

FEB 2

Daily Gratitude and Intention

Today I am grateful for:
- Balance perception of service to self = service to others
- Look in all areas of life

Today's Flip It:
- Balance perceived negative action/inaction until benefits = drawbacks
- Balance perceived positive action/inaction until drawbacks = benefits

My highest priority actions for tomorrow:

FEB 3

Being in the habit of saying "Thank you," of making sure that people receive attention so they know you value them, of not presuming that people will always be there—this is a good habit, regardless... make sure to give virtual and actual high-fives to those who rock and rock hard. — Sarah Wendell

Daily Gratitude and Intention

Today I am grateful for:
- Balance perception of service to self = service to others
- Look in all areas of life

Today's Flip It:
- Balance perceived negative action/inaction until benefits = drawbacks
- Balance perceived positive action/inaction until drawbacks = benefits

My highest priority actions for tomorrow:

Separate perceived negative actions/inactions from the person. The action is no more than a tool the person is using to try to get what they want. Choose to perceive the balance in the action and still love the person.
— Optimum Thinking

FEB 4

Daily Gratitude and Intention

Today I am grateful for:
- Balance perception of service to self = service to others
- Look in all areas of life

Today's Flip It:
- Balance perceived negative action/inaction until benefits = drawbacks
- Balance perceived positive action/inaction until drawbacks = benefits

My highest priority actions for tomorrow:

FEB 5

Can you see the holiness in those things you take for granted—a paved road or a washing machine? If you concentrate on finding what is good in every situation, you will discover that your life will suddenly be filled with gratitude, a feeling that nurtures the soul. — Rabbi Harold Kushner

Daily Gratitude and Intention

Today I am grateful for:
- Balance perception of service to self = service to others
- Look in all areas of life

Today's Flip It:
- Balance perceived negative action/inaction until benefits = drawbacks
- Balance perceived positive action/inaction until drawbacks = benefits

My highest priority actions for tomorrow:

How would you treat the environment when you have certainty that you will reincarnate repeatedly and never know who you will return as? — Optimum Thinking

FEB 6

Daily Gratitude and Intention

Today I am grateful for:
- Balance perception of service to self = service to others
- Look in all areas of life

Today's Flip It:
- Balance perceived negative action/inaction until benefits = drawbacks
- Balance perceived positive action/inaction until drawbacks = benefits

My highest priority actions for tomorrow:

FEB 7

> But the value of gratitude does not consist solely in getting you more blessings in the future. Without gratitude you cannot long keep from dissatisfied thought regarding things as they are.
> — Wallace Wattles

Daily Gratitude and Intention

Today I am grateful for:
- Balance perception of service to self = service to others
- Look in all areas of life

Today's Flip It:
- Balance perceived negative action/inaction until benefits = drawbacks
- Balance perceived positive action/inaction until drawbacks = benefits

My highest priority actions for tomorrow:

How would you treat other people and races when you have certainty that you will reincarnate repeatedly and never know who you will return as? — *Optimum Thinking*

FEB 8

Daily Gratitude and Intention

Today I am grateful for:
- Balance perception of service to self = service to others
- Look in all areas of life

Today's Flip It:
- Balance perceived negative action/inaction until benefits = drawbacks
- Balance perceived positive action/inaction until drawbacks = benefits

My highest priority actions for tomorrow:

FEB 9

Cultivate the habit of being grateful for every good thing that comes to you, and to give thanks continuously. And because all things have contributed to your advancement, you should include all things in your gratitude. — Ralph Waldo Emerson

Daily Gratitude and Intention

Today I am grateful for:
- Balance perception of service to self = service to others
- Look in all areas of life

Today's Flip It:
- Balance perceived negative action/inaction until benefits = drawbacks
- Balance perceived positive action/inaction until drawbacks = benefits

My highest priority actions for tomorrow:

We are all Double Agents of the Universe both supporting and challenging each other to transform and achieve our Optimum Life Missions. — Optimum Thinking

FEB 10

Daily Gratitude and Intention

Today I am grateful for:
- Balance perception of service to self = service to others
- Look in all areas of life

Today's Flip It:
- Balance perceived negative action/inaction until benefits = drawbacks
- Balance perceived positive action/inaction until drawbacks = benefits

My highest priority actions for tomorrow:

FEB 11

Do not take anything for granted — not one smile or one person or one rainbow or one breath, or one night in your cozy bed. — Terri Guillemets

Daily Gratitude and Intention

Today I am grateful for:
- Balance perception of service to self = service to others
- Look in all areas of life

Today's Flip It:
- Balance perceived negative action/inaction until benefits = drawbacks
- Balance perceived positive action/inaction until drawbacks = benefits

My highest priority actions for tomorrow:

Forget yesterday – it has already passed. Don't worry about tomorrow – you haven't got there yet. Open your heart with appreciation to the present – it is your most valuable gift.
— *Optimum Thinking*

FEB 12

Daily Gratitude and Intention

Today I am grateful for:
- Balance perception of service to self = service to others
- Look in all areas of life

Today's Flip It:
- Balance perceived negative action/inaction until benefits = drawbacks
- Balance perceived positive action/inaction until drawbacks = benefits

My highest priority actions for tomorrow:

FEB 13

Develop an attitude of gratitude, and give thanks for everything that happens to you, knowing that every step forward is a step toward achieving something bigger and better than your current situation. — Brian Tracy

Daily Gratitude and Intention

Today I am grateful for:
- Balance perception of service to self = service to others
- Look in all areas of life

Today's Flip It:
- Balance perceived negative action/inaction until benefits = drawbacks
- Balance perceived positive action/inaction until drawbacks = benefits

My highest priority actions for tomorrow:

Completing your annual and monthly planning is a powerful way to assess what is really important to you. You will have real evidence of where you actually have choosen to invest your resources and help you clarify what you want moving forward.
— Optimum Thinking

FEB 14

Daily Gratitude and Intention

Today I am grateful for:
- Balance perception of service to self = service to others
- Look in all areas of life

Today's Flip It:
- Balance perceived negative action/inaction until benefits = drawbacks
- Balance perceived positive action/inaction until drawbacks = benefits

My highest priority actions for tomorrow:

FEB 15

Do not spoil what you have by desiring what you have not; remember that what you now have was once among the things you only hoped for.
— Epicurus

Daily Gratitude and Intention

Today I am grateful for:
- Balance perception of service to self = service to others
- Look in all areas of life

Today's Flip It:
- Balance perceived negative action/inaction until benefits = drawbacks
- Balance perceived positive action/inaction until drawbacks = benefits

My highest priority actions for tomorrow:

People who act like an Underdog and play small will attact challenging circumstances to kick them back into action and growth. — Optimum Thinking

FEB 16

Daily Gratitude and Intention

Today I am grateful for:
- Balance perception of service to self = service to others
- Look in all areas of life

Today's Flip It:
- Balance perceived negative action/inaction until benefits = drawbacks
- Balance perceived positive action/inaction until drawbacks = benefits

My highest priority actions for tomorrow:

FEB 17

Don't count your blessings, let your blessings count! EnjoyLife! — Bernard Kelvin Clive

Daily Gratitude and Intention

Today I am grateful for:
- Balance perception of service to self = service to others
- Look in all areas of life

Today's Flip It:
- Balance perceived negative action/inaction until benefits = drawbacks
- Balance perceived positive action/inaction until drawbacks = benefits

My highest priority actions for tomorrow:

You program yourself with the words you use. Watch out for "victim language". When you blame others for what you have attracted into your life you are giving your power away. If you have attracted challenges there are benefits in it for you, if you take the time to think hard and find them.
— Optimum Thinking

Daily Gratitude and Intention

Today I am grateful for:
- Balance perception of service to self = service to others
- Look in all areas of life

Today's Flip It:
- Balance perceived negative action/inaction until benefits = drawbacks
- Balance perceived positive action/inaction until drawbacks = benefits

My highest priority actions for tomorrow:

FEB 19

Enjoy the little things, for one day you may look back and realize they were the big thing. — Robert Brault

Daily Gratitude and Intention

Today I am grateful for:
- Balance perception of service to self = service to others
- Look in all areas of life

Today's Flip It:
- Balance perceived negative action/inaction until benefits = drawbacks
- Balance perceived positive action/inaction until drawbacks = benefits

My highest priority actions for tomorrow:

If you seek a life that is happy all of the time, you are setting yourself up for failure. Instead seek a fulfilled life where you embrace both challenge and support to get what you want. — Optimum Thinking

FEB 20

Daily Gratitude and Intention

Today I am grateful for:
- Balance perception of service to self = service to others
- Look in all areas of life

Today's Flip It:
- Balance perceived negative action/inaction until benefits = drawbacks
- Balance perceived positive action/inaction until drawbacks = benefits

My highest priority actions for tomorrow:

FEB 21

Enough is a feast. — Buddhist Proverb

Daily Gratitude and Intention

Today I am grateful for:
- Balance perception of service to self = service to others
- Look in all areas of life

Today's Flip It:
- Balance perceived negative action/inaction until benefits = drawbacks
- Balance perceived positive action/inaction until drawbacks = benefits

My highest priority actions for tomorrow:

> There is only one person who can give you "self-esteem". If you are beating yourself up, find where you know you have skills and abilities that are above other people until you perceive you are equal to others and perfectly, uniquely you. — Optimum Thinking

FEB 22

Daily Gratitude and Intention

Today I am grateful for:
- Balance perception of service to self = service to others
- Look in all areas of life

Today's Flip It:
- Balance perceived negative action/inaction until benefits = drawbacks
- Balance perceived positive action/inaction until drawbacks = benefits

My highest priority actions for tomorrow:

FEB 23

Gratitude is a magnet that aligns you to who you innately are. — Sajeela Cormack

Daily Gratitude and Intention

Today I am grateful for:
- Balance perception of service to self = service to others
- Look in all areas of life

Today's Flip It:
- Balance perceived negative action/inaction until benefits = drawbacks
- Balance perceived positive action/inaction until drawbacks = benefits

My highest priority actions for tomorrow:

> There is a divine intelligence that is beyond our comprehension that is running this show we call life. The wisdom of this intelligence has set us up to strive to achieve, learn and grow. When you are wallowing in a 'pity party' you have forgotten your purpose and what it will take to achieve it. Set goals and get your hands back on the steering wheel of your life!
> — Optimum Thinking

FEB 24

Daily Gratitude and Intention

Today I am grateful for:
- Balance perception of service to self = service to others
- Look in all areas of life

Today's Flip It:
- Balance perceived negative action/inaction until benefits = drawbacks
- Balance perceived positive action/inaction until drawbacks = benefits

My highest priority actions for tomorrow:

FEB 25

Everyone creates realities based on their own personal beliefs. These beliefs are so powerful that they can create [expansive or entrapping] realities over and over.
— Kuan Yin

Daily Gratitude and Intention

Today I am grateful for:
- Balance perception of service to self = service to others
- Look in all areas of life

Today's Flip It:
- Balance perceived negative action/inaction until benefits = drawbacks
- Balance perceived positive action/inaction until drawbacks = benefits

My highest priority actions for tomorrow:

When a parent sets a boundary for their child, it is because they love them enough to do something the child may perceive as 'bad'. Understanding boundaries is critical for us to live as a family and society. — **Optimum Thinking**

FEB 26

Daily Gratitude and Intention

Today I am grateful for:
- Balance perception of service to self = service to others
- Look in all areas of life

Today's Flip It:
- Balance perceived negative action/inaction until benefits = drawbacks
- Balance perceived positive action/inaction until drawbacks = benefits

My highest priority actions for tomorrow:

FEB 27

Fearing to lose what you have is not the same as appreciation. You have to take a step beyond that.
— Terri Guillemets

Daily Gratitude and Intention

Today I am grateful for:
- Balance perception of service to self = service to others
- Look in all areas of life

Today's Flip It:
- Balance perceived negative action/inaction until benefits = drawbacks
- Balance perceived positive action/inaction until drawbacks = benefits

My highest priority actions for tomorrow:

If you are not achieving a goal, assess why you haven't. If it is too big, break it down into smaller steps. If it is not important enough to you, delete it. Live the life you consciously choose!
— Optimum Thinking

FEB 28

Daily Gratitude and Intention

Today I am grateful for:
- Balance perception of service to self = service to others
- Look in all areas of life.

Today's Flip It:
- Balance perceived negative action/inaction until benefits = drawbacks
- Balance perceived positive action/inaction until drawbacks = benefits

My highest priority actions for tomorrow:

FEB 29

Feeling gratitude and not expressing it is like wrapping a present and not giving it. – William Arthur Ward

Daily Gratitude and Intention

Today I am grateful for:
- Balance perception of service to self = service to others
- Look in all areas of life

Today's Flip It:
- Balance perceived negative action/inaction until benefits = drawbacks
- Balance perceived positive action/inaction until drawbacks = benefits

My highest priority actions for tomorrow:

MARCH

Monthly Intention Plan

Write the top priorities you intend to focus on in each area of your life during this month.

SPIRITUAL / MISSION / SELF-ACTUALIZATION

MENTAL / EDUCATION

VOCATION / CAREER

FINANCIAL WEALTH / SAVING & INVESTING

FAMILY / RELATIONSHIP

SOCIAL / FRIENDS

HEALTH & PHYSICAL APPEARANCE

MAR 1

Feeling grateful or appreciative of someone or something in your life actually attracts more of the things that you appreciate and value into your life. — Christiane Northrup

Daily Gratitude and Intention

Today I am grateful for:
- Balance perception of service to self = service to others
- Look in all areas of life

Today's Flip It:
- Balance perceived negative action/inaction until benefits = drawbacks
- Balance perceived positive action/inaction until drawbacks = benefits

My highest priority actions for tomorrow:

You live your Optimum Life when you consciously choose what you want, plan how to get it and learn to clear emotional charge that gets in the way. — Optimum Thinking

MAR 2

Daily Gratitude and Intention

Today I am grateful for:
- Balance perception of service to self = service to others
- Look in all areas of life

Today's Flip It:
- Balance perceived negative action/inaction until benefits = drawbacks
- Balance perceived positive action/inaction until drawbacks = benefits

My highest priority actions for tomorrow:

MAR 3

Understand your Hierarchy of Individual Life Priorities (HILP).
"When you are content to be simply yourself and don't compare or compete, everybody will respect you." — Lao Tzu

Daily Gratitude and Intention

Today I am grateful for:
- Balance perception of service to self = service to others
- Look in all areas of life

Today's Flip It:
- Balance perceived negative action/inaction until benefits = drawbacks
- Balance perceived positive action/inaction until drawbacks = benefits

My highest priority actions for tomorrow:

If you perceive something is "too good to be true" then it is time to do some work and find all of the drawbacks to it until you can see it has both sides equally. If you don't, you will be gullible and likely to be overpowered in some way.
— Optimum Thinking

MAR 4

Daily Gratitude and Intention

Today I am grateful for:
- Balance perception of service to self = service to others
- Look in all areas of life

Today's Flip It:
- Balance perceived negative action/inaction until benefits = drawbacks
- Balance perceived positive action/inaction until drawbacks = benefits

My highest priority actions for tomorrow:

MAR 5

Gratitude is an opener of locked-up blessings.
— Marianne Williamson

Daily Gratitude and Intention

Today I am grateful for:
- Balance perception of service to self = service to others
- Look in all areas of life

Today's Flip It:
- Balance perceived negative action/inaction until benefits = drawbacks
- Balance perceived positive action/inaction until drawbacks = benefits

My highest priority actions for tomorrow:

Life wasn't meant to be easy. It is meant to be fulfilling. You will never feel fulfilled if you haven't set yourself challenges and overcome them! — Optimum Thinking

MAR 6

Daily Gratitude and Intention

Today I am grateful for:
- Balance perception of service to self = service to others
- Look in all areas of life

Today's Flip It:
- Balance perceived negative action/inaction until benefits = drawbacks
- Balance perceived positive action/inaction until drawbacks = benefits

My highest priority actions for tomorrow:

MAR 7

Forget yesterday—it has already forgotten you. Don't sweat tomorrow—you haven't even met. Instead, open your eyes and your heart to a truly precious gift—today.
— Steve Maraboli

Daily Gratitude and Intention

Today I am grateful for:
- Balance perception of service to self = service to others
- Look in all areas of life

Today's Flip It:
- Balance perceived negative action/inaction until benefits = drawbacks
- Balance perceived positive action/inaction until drawbacks = benefits

My highest priority actions for tomorrow:

If you perceive you had a boring day today, think about what you may have missed out on by not managing your emotional state and intention. — Optimum Thinking

MAR 8

Daily Gratitude and Intention

Today I am grateful for:
- Balance perception of service to self = service to others
- Look in all areas of life

Today's Flip It:
- Balance perceived negative action/inaction until benefits = drawbacks
- Balance perceived positive action/inaction until drawbacks = benefits

My highest priority actions for tomorrow:

MAR 9

Give thanks for a little and you will find a lot.
— The Hausa of Nigeria

Daily Gratitude and Intention

Today I am grateful for:
- Balance perception of service to self = service to others
- Look in all areas of life

Today's Flip It:
- Balance perceived negative action/inaction until benefits = drawbacks
- Balance perceived positive action/inaction until drawbacks = benefits

My highest priority actions for tomorrow:

Optimum Thinking skills take work. The more you put in, the more you accelerate your achievements and relationships. — *Optimum Thinking*

MAR 10

Daily Gratitude and Intention

Today I am grateful for:
- Balance perception of service to self = service to others
- Look in all areas of life

Today's Flip It:
- Balance perceived negative action/inaction until benefits = drawbacks
- Balance perceived positive action/inaction until drawbacks = benefits

My highest priority actions for tomorrow:

MAR 11

God gave you a gift of 86,400 seconds today. Have you used one to say "thank you?" — William A. Ward

Daily Gratitude and Intention

Today I am grateful for:
- Balance perception of service to self = service to others
- Look in all areas of life

Today's Flip It:
- Balance perceived negative action/inaction until benefits = drawbacks
- Balance perceived positive action/inaction until drawbacks = benefits

My highest priority actions for tomorrow:

Plan your Optimum Life and live your love. Don't blame other people for not getting what you want. They are all busy working on getting what they want! — Optimum Thinking

MAR 12

Daily Gratitude and Intention

Today I am grateful for:
- Balance perception of service to self = service to others
- Look in all areas of life

Today's Flip It:
- Balance perceived negative action/inaction until benefits = drawbacks
- Balance perceived positive action/inaction until drawbacks = benefits

My highest priority actions for tomorrow:

MAR 13

Grace isn't a little prayer you chant before receiving a meal. It's a way to live.
— Attributed to Jacqueline Winspear

Daily Gratitude and Intention

Today I am grateful for:
- Balance perception of service to self = service to others
- Look in all areas of life

Today's Flip It:
- Balance perceived negative action/inaction until benefits = drawbacks
- Balance perceived positive action/inaction until drawbacks = benefits

My highest priority actions for tomorrow:

Our language is full of polarization that encourages emotional reactions. Try using hyphens to find more balanced language e.g. humbly-empowered. — Optimum Thinking

MAR 14

Daily Gratitude and Intention

Today I am grateful for:
- Balance perception of service to self = service to others
- Look in all areas of life

Today's Flip It:
- Balance perceived negative action/inaction until benefits = drawbacks
- Balance perceived positive action/inaction until drawbacks = benefits

My highest priority actions for tomorrow:

MAR 15

Gratitude also opens your eyes to the limitless potential of the universe, while dissatisfaction closes your eyes to it. — Stephen Richards

Daily Gratitude and Intention

Today I am grateful for:
- Balance perception of service to self = service to others
- Look in all areas of life

Today's Flip It:
- Balance perceived negative action/inaction until benefits = drawbacks
- Balance perceived positive action/inaction until drawbacks = benefits

My highest priority actions for tomorrow:

Gratitude, joy, inspiration and enthusiasm are the emotional states of an open heart. — Optimum Thinking

MAR 16

Daily Gratitude and Intention

Today I am grateful for:
- Balance perception of service to self = service to others
- Look in all areas of life

Today's Flip It:
- Balance perceived negative action/inaction until benefits = drawbacks
- Balance perceived positive action/inaction until drawbacks = benefits

My highest priority actions for tomorrow:

MAR 17

Life is very interesting ... in the end, some of your greatest pains become your greatest strenghts.
— Drew Barrymore

Daily Gratitude and Intention

Today I am grateful for:
- Balance perception of service to self = service to others
- Look in all areas of life

Today's Flip It:
- Balance perceived negative action/inaction until benefits = drawbacks
- Balance perceived positive action/inaction until drawbacks = benefits

My highest priority actions for tomorrow:

Overdogs have care-less relationships. Underdogs are too care-ful in relationships and feel like they are treading on egg shells. Optimum dogs have caring relationships. They see their partner as equal and both challenge and support them to grow and achieve. — *Optimum Thinking*

MAR 18

Daily Gratitude and Intention

Today I am grateful for:
- Balance perception of service to self = service to others
- Look in all areas of life

Today's Flip It:
- Balance perceived negative action/inaction until benefits = drawbacks
- Balance perceived positive action/inaction until drawbacks = benefits

My highest priority actions for tomorrow:

MAR 19

Gratitude bestows reverence, allowing us to encounter everyday epiphanies, those transcendent moments of awe that change forever how we experience life and the world. — John Milton

Daily Gratitude and Intention

Today I am grateful for:
- Balance perception of service to self = service to others
- Look in all areas of life

Today's Flip It:
- Balance perceived negative action/inaction until benefits = drawbacks
- Balance perceived positive action/inaction until drawbacks = benefits

My highest priority actions for tomorrow:

Don't waste time comparing yourself to other people. Look within and you will find all of the talents you need to fulfil your true purpose and Optimum Life Mission. — Optimum Thinking

MAR 20

Daily Gratitude and Intention

Today I am grateful for:
- Balance perception of service to self = service to others
- Look in all areas of life

Today's Flip It:
- Balance perceived negative action/inaction until benefits = drawbacks
- Balance perceived positive action/inaction until drawbacks = benefits

My highest priority actions for tomorrow:

MAR 21

Gratitude can transform common days into thanksgivings, turn routine jobs into joy, and change ordinary opportunities into blessings.
— William Arthur Ward

Daily Gratitude and Intention

Today I am grateful for:
- Balance perception of service to self = service to others
- Look in all areas of life

Today's Flip It:
- Balance perceived negative action/inaction until benefits = drawbacks
- Balance perceived positive action/inaction until drawbacks = benefits

My highest priority actions for tomorrow:

> When you feel angry about something someone did to you, ask yourself how what they did will help you achieve what is important to you until you perceive the benefits are equal to the drawbacks. — *Optimum Thinking*

MAR 22

Daily Gratitude and Intention

Today I am grateful for:
- Balance perception of service to self = service to others
- Look in all areas of life

Today's Flip It:
- Balance perceived negative action/inaction until benefits = drawbacks
- Balance perceived positive action/inaction until drawbacks = benefits

My highest priority actions for tomorrow:

MAR 23

An ant on the move does more than a dozing ox.
— Lao Tzu

Daily Gratitude and Intention

Today I am grateful for:
- Balance perception of service to self = service to others
- Look in all areas of life

Today's Flip It:
- Balance perceived negative action/inaction until benefits = drawbacks
- Balance perceived positive action/inaction until drawbacks = benefits

My highest priority actions for tomorrow:

The most powerful state of attraction is gratitude.
— *Optimum Thinking*

MAR 24

Daily Gratitude and Intention

Today I am grateful for:
- Balance perception of service to self = service to others
- Look in all areas of life

Today's Flip It:
- Balance perceived negative action/inaction until benefits = drawbacks
- Balance perceived positive action/inaction until drawbacks = benefits

My highest priority actions for tomorrow:

MAR 25

Gratitude helps you to grow and expand; gratitude brings joy and laughter into your life and into the lives of all those around you. — Eileen Caddy

Daily Gratitude and Intention

Today I am grateful for:
- Balance perception of service to self = service to others
- Look in all areas of life

Today's Flip It:
- Balance perceived negative action/inaction until benefits = drawbacks
- Balance perceived positive action/inaction until drawbacks = benefits

My highest priority actions for tomorrow:

> You are the only person who can inspire you – it is a feeling in your heart. You are in control of your emotional state. What emotional state do you want to create today? — *Optimum Thinking*

MAR 26

Daily Gratitude and Intention

Today I am grateful for:
- Balance perception of service to self = service to others
- Look in all areas of life

Today's Flip It:
- Balance perceived negative action/inaction until benefits = drawbacks
- Balance perceived positive action/inaction until drawbacks = benefits

My highest priority actions for tomorrow:

MAR 27

Gratitude is a quality similar to electricity: it must be produced and discharged and used up in order to exist at all. — William Faulkner

Daily Gratitude and Intention

Today I am grateful for:
- Balance perception of service to self = service to others
- Look in all areas of life

Today's Flip It:
- Balance perceived negative action/inaction until benefits = drawbacks
- Balance perceived positive action/inaction until drawbacks = benefits

My highest priority actions for tomorrow:

> *When you feel guilty about something you did to someone, ask yourself how what you did helped them achieve what is important to them until you perceive the benefits to them are equal to the drawbacks.* — Optimum Thinking

MAR 28

Daily Gratitude and Intention

Today I am grateful for:
- Balance perception of service to self = service to others
- Look in all areas of life

Today's Flip It:
- Balance perceived negative action/inaction until benefits = drawbacks
- Balance perceived positive action/inaction until drawbacks = benefits

My highest priority actions for tomorrow:

MAR 29

Gratitude is a vaccine, an antitoxin, and an antiseptic. — John Henry Jowett

Daily Gratitude and Intention

Today I am grateful for:
- Balance perception of service to self = service to others
- Look in all areas of life

Today's Flip It:
- Balance perceived negative action/inaction until benefits = drawbacks
- Balance perceived positive action/inaction until drawbacks = benefits

My highest priority actions for tomorrow:

Optimum Thinking ... when positive thinking just isn't enough. — Optimum Thinking

MAR 30

Daily Gratitude and Intention

Today I am grateful for:
- Balance perception of service to self = service to others
- Look in all areas of life

Today's Flip It:
- Balance perceived negative action/inaction until benefits = drawbacks
- Balance perceived positive action/inaction until drawbacks = benefits

My highest priority actions for tomorrow:

MAR 31

Gratitude requires both heart and mind to be engaged, and paves the road to fulfilment.
— *Optimum Thinking*

Daily Gratitude and Intention

Today I am grateful for:
- Balance perception of service to self = service to others
- Look in all areas of life

Today's Flip It:
- Balance perceived negative action/inaction until benefits = drawbacks
- Balance perceived positive action/inaction until drawbacks = benefits

My highest priority actions for tomorrow:

APRIL

Monthly Intention Plan

Write the top priorities you intend to focus on in each area of your life during this month.

SPIRITUAL / MISSION / SELF-ACTUALIZATION

MENTAL / EDUCATION

VOCATION / CAREER

FINANCIAL WEALTH / SAVING & INVESTING

FAMILY / RELATIONSHIP

SOCIAL / FRIENDS

HEALTH & PHYSICAL APPEARANCE

APR 1

Gratitude is an art of painting an adversity into a lovely picture. — Kak Sri

Daily Gratitude and Intention

Today I am grateful for:
- Balance perception of service to self = service to others
- Look in all areas of life

Today's Flip It:
- Balance perceived negative action/inaction until benefits = drawbacks
- Balance perceived positive action/inaction until drawbacks = benefits

My highest priority actions for tomorrow:

You have programmed yourself with your beliefs. Bring to mind as many as you can and check if they empower or disempower you. — Optimum Thinking

APR 2

Daily Gratitude and Intention

Today I am grateful for:
- Balance perception of service to self = service to others
- Look in all areas of life

Today's Flip It:
- Balance perceived negative action/inaction until benefits = drawbacks
- Balance perceived positive action/inaction until drawbacks = benefits

My highest priority actions for tomorrow:

APR 3

Gratitude is one of the sweet shortcuts to finding peace of mind and happiness inside. No matter what is going on outside of us, there's always something we could be grateful for.
— Barry Neil Kaufman

Daily Gratitude and Intention

Today I am grateful for:
- Balance perception of service to self = service to others
- Look in all areas of life

Today's Flip It:
- Balance perceived negative action/inaction until benefits = drawbacks
- Balance perceived positive action/inaction until drawbacks = benefits

My highest priority actions for tomorrow:

You change disempowering beliefs by finding new data that supports a more empowering belief. You adopt the new belief once you have enough data to convince yourself of the new belief. — Optimum Thinking

APR 4

Daily Gratitude and Intention

Today I am grateful for:
- Balance perception of service to self = service to others
- Look in all areas of life

Today's Flip It:
- Balance perceived negative action/inaction until benefits = drawbacks
- Balance perceived positive action/inaction until drawbacks = benefits

My highest priority actions for tomorrow:

APR 5

Gratitude is least articulate when it is felt most deeply. — Optimum Thinking

Daily Gratitude and Intention

Today I am grateful for:
- Balance perception of service to self = service to others
- Look in all areas of life

Today's Flip It:
- Balance perceived negative action/inaction until benefits = drawbacks
- Balance perceived positive action/inaction until drawbacks = benefits

My highest priority actions for tomorrow:

Observe groups who are operating in a highly productive manner and notice how they are supporting and challenging each other to achieve what they want. You will become more aware of what creates conflict in future situations. — Optimum Thinking

APR 6

Daily Gratitude and Intention

Today I am grateful for:
- Balance perception of service to self = service to others
- Look in all areas of life

Today's Flip It:
- Balance perceived negative action/inaction until benefits = drawbacks
- Balance perceived positive action/inaction until drawbacks = benefits

My highest priority actions for tomorrow:

APR 7

Gratitude is the ability to experience life as a gift. It liberates us from the prison of self-preoccupation.
— John Ortberg

Daily Gratitude and Intention

Today I am grateful for:
- Balance perception of service to self = service to others
- Look in all areas of life

Today's Flip It:
- Balance perceived negative action/inaction until benefits = drawbacks
- Balance perceived positive action/inaction until drawbacks = benefits

My highest priority actions for tomorrow:

Be grateful for your negative thinking; it is designed to help you work out what you DON'T want.
— Optimum Thinking

APR 8

Daily Gratitude and Intention

Today I am grateful for:
- Balance perception of service to self = service to others
- Look in all areas of life

Today's Flip It:
- Balance perceived negative action/inaction until benefits = drawbacks
- Balance perceived positive action/inaction until drawbacks = benefits

My highest priority actions for tomorrow:

APR 9

Gratitude is riches. Complaint is poverty. — Doris Day

Daily Gratitude and Intention

Today I am grateful for:
- Balance perception of service to self = service to others
- Look in all areas of life

Today's Flip It:
- Balance perceived negative action/inaction until benefits = drawbacks
- Balance perceived positive action/inaction until drawbacks = benefits

My highest priority actions for tomorrow:

> If, at the end of a day you are feeling really proud enjoy it for a moment and then ask yourself who you could have served better today to bring yourself back to being equal to others (Optimum Dog) before you attract external humbling circumstances to do it for you. — *Optimum Thinking*

APR 10

Daily Gratitude and Intention

Today I am grateful for:
- Balance perception of service to self = service to others
- Look in all areas of life

Today's Flip It:
- Balance perceived negative action/inaction until benefits = drawbacks
- Balance perceived positive action/inaction until drawbacks = benefits

My highest priority actions for tomorrow:

APR 11

Gratitude is the sign of noble souls. — Aesop

Daily Gratitude and Intention

Today I am grateful for:
- Balance perception of service to self = service to others
- Look in all areas of life

Today's Flip It:
- Balance perceived negative action/inaction until benefits = drawbacks
- Balance perceived positive action/inaction until drawbacks = benefits

My highest priority actions for tomorrow:

When you feel a strong negative emotional charge, first ask yourself what unrealistic expectations you may have in that moment. — Optimum Thinking

APR 12

Daily Gratitude and Intention

Today I am grateful for:
- Balance perception of service to self = service to others
- Look in all areas of life

....
....
....
....
....
....
....
....
....
....
....
....

Today's Flip It:
- Balance perceived negative action/inaction until benefits = drawbacks
- Balance perceived positive action/inaction until drawbacks = benefits

....
....
....
....
....
....

My highest priority actions for tomorrow:
....
....
....
....
....

APR 13

Gratitude is the fairest blossom which springs from the soul. — Henry Ward Beecher

Daily Gratitude and Intention

Today I am grateful for:
- Balance perception of service to self = service to others
- Look in all areas of life

Today's Flip It:
- Balance perceived negative action/inaction until benefits = drawbacks
- Balance perceived positive action/inaction until drawbacks = benefits

My highest priority actions for tomorrow:

> *If you want to create and sustain connected meaningful relationships, make sure you understand each other's goals so you can support their achievement and they can support yours.* — Optimum Thinking

APR 14

Daily Gratitude and Intention

Today I am grateful for:
- Balance perception of service to self = service to others
- Look in all areas of life

Today's Flip It:
- Balance perceived negative action/inaction until benefits = drawbacks
- Balance perceived positive action/inaction until drawbacks = benefits

My highest priority actions for tomorrow:

APR 15

Gratitude is the state of mind of thankfulness. As it is cultivated, we experience an increase in our "sympathetic joy," our happiness at another's happiness.
— Stephen Levine

Daily Gratitude and Intention

Today I am grateful for:
- Balance perception of service to self = service to others
- Look in all areas of life

Today's Flip It:
- Balance perceived negative action/inaction until benefits = drawbacks
- Balance perceived positive action/inaction until drawbacks = benefits

My highest priority actions for tomorrow:

Be grateful for the people and friends who have left your life and made space for the new people who have come in to support and challenge you to keep growing. — Optimum Thinking

APR 16

Daily Gratitude and Intention

Today I am grateful for:
- Balance perception of service to self = service to others
- Look in all areas of life

....

Today's Flip It:
- Balance perceived negative action/inaction until benefits = drawbacks
- Balance perceived positive action/inaction until drawbacks = benefits

....

My highest priority actions for tomorrow:

....

APR 17

Gratitude is the memory of the heart.
— Jean Baptiste Massieu

Daily Gratitude and Intention

Today I am grateful for:
- Balance perception of service to self = service to others
- Look in all areas of life

Today's Flip It:
- Balance perceived negative action/inaction until benefits = drawbacks
- Balance perceived positive action/inaction until drawbacks = benefits

My highest priority actions for tomorrow:

Nothing is ever gained or lost; it changes form. If you perceive you have lost someone or some thing, find the new forms you now have it in to see that you continue to have what you want in your life.
— Optimum Thinking

APR 18

Daily Gratitude and Intention

Today I am grateful for:
- Balance perception of service to self = service to others
- Look in all areas of life

Today's Flip It:
- Balance perceived negative action/inaction until benefits = drawbacks
- Balance perceived positive action/inaction until drawbacks = benefits

My highest priority actions for tomorrow:

APR 19

What if you gave someone a gift, and they neglected to thank you for it — would you be likely to give them another? Life is the same way. In order to attract more of the blessings that life has to offer, you must truly appreciate what you already have.
— Ralph Marston

Daily Gratitude and Intention

Today I am grateful for:
- Balance perception of service to self = service to others
- Look in all areas of life

Today's Flip It:
- Balance perceived negative action/inaction until benefits = drawbacks
- Balance perceived positive action/inaction until drawbacks = benefits

My highest priority actions for tomorrow:

If you fight too hard to have something it will elude you until you appreciate what you have. If you fight too hard to avoid something, you will attract it until you learn to appreciate it. — Optimum Thinking

APR 20

Daily Gratitude and Intention

Today I am grateful for:
- Balance perception of service to self = service to others
- Look in all areas of life

Today's Flip It:
- Balance perceived negative action/inaction until benefits = drawbacks
- Balance perceived positive action/inaction until drawbacks = benefits

My highest priority actions for tomorrow:

APR 21

Energy and vitality are infinite when you recognize and appreciate their source: a heart filled with gratitude.
— John Demartini

Daily Gratitude and Intention

Today I am grateful for:
- Balance perception of service to self = service to others
- Look in all areas of life

Today's Flip It:
- Balance perceived negative action/inaction until benefits = drawbacks
- Balance perceived positive action/inaction until drawbacks = benefits

My highest priority actions for tomorrow:

> *Goals need to connect with your heart, push your current capacity and be big enough to scare you a little. Then you need to make your plan clear and detailed enough to inspire you into focussed action.*
> — Optimum Thinking

APR 22

Daily Gratitude and Intention

Today I am grateful for:
- Balance perception of service to self = service to others
- Look in all areas of life

Today's Flip It:
- Balance perceived negative action/inaction until benefits = drawbacks
- Balance perceived positive action/inaction until drawbacks = benefits

My highest priority actions for tomorrow:

APR 23

Gratitude is the sweetest thing in a seeker's life—in all human life. If there is gratitude in your heart, then there will be tremendous sweetness in your eyes. — Sri Chinmoy

Daily Gratitude and Intention

Today I am grateful for:
- Balance perception of service to self = service to others
- Look in all areas of life

Today's Flip It:
- Balance perceived negative action/inaction until benefits = drawbacks
- Balance perceived positive action/inaction until drawbacks = benefits

My highest priority actions for tomorrow:

The only "perfect" you are meant to be is "perfectly you"! That is something only you can achieve. — Optimum Thinking

APR 24

Daily Gratitude and Intention

Today I am grateful for:
- Balance perception of service to self = service to others
- Look in all areas of life

....
....
....
....
....
....
....
....
....
....
....
....

Today's Flip It:
- Balance perceived negative action/inaction until benefits = drawbacks
- Balance perceived positive action/inaction until drawbacks = benefits

....
....
....
....
....
....

My highest priority actions for tomorrow:

....
....
....
....
....

APR 25

Gratitude takes the negative emotional charge out of anger. — Optimum Thinking

Daily Gratitude and Intention

Today I am grateful for:
- Balance perception of service to self = service to others
- Look in all areas of life

Today's Flip It:
- Balance perceived negative action/inaction until benefits = drawbacks
- Balance perceived positive action/inaction until drawbacks = benefits

My highest priority actions for tomorrow:

Negative emotions hurt you! Every time you hate someone; as you release harmful stress chemicals from your brain to your body, you truly hate yourself!
— Optimum Thinking

APR 26

Daily Gratitude and Intention

Today I am grateful for:
- Balance perception of service to self = service to others
- Look in all areas of life

Today's Flip It:
- Balance perceived negative action/inaction until benefits = drawbacks
- Balance perceived positive action/inaction until drawbacks = benefits

My highest priority actions for tomorrow:

APR 27

Gratitude makes sense of our past, brings peace for today, and creates a vision for tomorrow.
— Melody Beattie

Daily Gratitude and Intention

Today I am grateful for:
- Balance perception of service to self = service to others
- Look in all areas of life

Today's Flip It:
- Balance perceived negative action/inaction until benefits = drawbacks
- Balance perceived positive action/inaction until drawbacks = benefits

My highest priority actions for tomorrow:

> When conflict occurs, get curious about what each person's agenda really is and you will understand their behaviour more easily. Think about what each person has as their Hierarchy of Individual Life Priorities (HILP) and what is being challenged in that moment.
> — Optimum Thinking

APR 28

Daily Gratitude and Intention

Today I am grateful for:
- Balance perception of service to self = service to others
- Look in all areas of life

Today's Flip It:
- Balance perceived negative action/inaction until benefits = drawbacks
- Balance perceived positive action/inaction until drawbacks = benefits

My highest priority actions for tomorrow:

APR 29

Gratitude should not be just a reaction to getting what you want, but an all-the-time gratitude, the kind where you notice the little things and where you constantly look for the good, even in unpleasant situations. Start bringing gratitude to your experiences, instead of waiting for a positive experience in order to feel grateful. — Marelisa Fábrega

Daily Gratitude and Intention

Today I am grateful for:
- Balance perception of service to self = service to others
- Look in all areas of life

Today's Flip It:
- Balance perceived negative action/inaction until benefits = drawbacks
- Balance perceived positive action/inaction until drawbacks = benefits

My highest priority actions for tomorrow:

> Optimum Thinking harnesses the power of positive and negative thinking to see how an event is perfect for us at that time to help us grow and learn.
> — Optimum Thinking

APR 30

Daily Gratitude and Intention

Today I am grateful for:
- Balance perception of service to self = service to others
- Look in all areas of life

Today's Flip It:
- Balance perceived negative action/inaction until benefits = drawbacks
- Balance perceived positive action/inaction until drawbacks = benefits

My highest priority actions for tomorrow:

MAY

Monthly Intention Plan

Write the top priorities you intend to focus on in each area of your life during this month.

SPIRITUAL / MISSION / SELF-ACTUALIZATION

MENTAL / EDUCATION

VOCATION / CAREER

FINANCIAL WEALTH / SAVING & INVESTING

FAMILY / RELATIONSHIP

SOCIAL / FRIENDS

HEALTH & PHYSICAL APPEARANCE

MAY 1

Gratitude turns what we have into enough, and more. It turns denial into acceptance, chaos into order and confusion into clarity. It can turn a meal into a feast, a house into a home, a stranger into a friend. — Melody Beattie

Daily Gratitude and Intention

Today I am grateful for:
- Balance perception of service to self = service to others
- Look in all areas of life

Today's Flip It:
- Balance perceived negative action/inaction until benefits = drawbacks
- Balance perceived positive action/inaction until drawbacks = benefits

My highest priority actions for tomorrow:

Your level of frustration for not achieving is in direct proportion to your lack of planning. — Optimum Thinking

MAY 2

Daily Gratitude and Intention

Today I am grateful for:
- Balance perception of service to self = service to others
- Look in all areas of life

Today's Flip It:
- Balance perceived negative action/inaction until benefits = drawbacks
- Balance perceived positive action/inaction until drawbacks = benefits

My highest priority actions for tomorrow:

MAY 3

Happiness cannot be traveled to, owned, earned, worn or consumed. Happiness is the spiritual experience of living every minute with love, grace, and gratitude. — Denis Waitley

Daily Gratitude and Intention

Today I am grateful for:
- Balance perception of service to self = service to others
- Look in all areas of life

Today's Flip It:
- Balance perceived negative action/inaction until benefits = drawbacks
- Balance perceived positive action/inaction until drawbacks = benefits

My highest priority actions for tomorrow:

If you just set out to be liked, you would be prepared to compromise on anything at any time, and you would achieve nothing. — Margaret Thatcher

MAY 4

Daily Gratitude and Intention

Today I am grateful for:
- Balance perception of service to self = service to others
- Look in all areas of life

Today's Flip It:
- Balance perceived negative action/inaction until benefits = drawbacks
- Balance perceived positive action/inaction until drawbacks = benefits

My highest priority actions for tomorrow:

MAY 5

Hem your blessings with thankfulness so they don't unravel.
— Author Unknown

Daily Gratitude and Intention

Today I am grateful for:
- Balance perception of service to self = service to others
- Look in all areas of life

Today's Flip It:
- Balance perceived negative action/inaction until benefits = drawbacks
- Balance perceived positive action/inaction until drawbacks = benefits

My highest priority actions for tomorrow:

People stay in quality relationships when they are both truly grateful for how they support and challenge each other to connect, grow and achieve their highest individual life priorities. — Optimum Thinking

MAY 6

Daily Gratitude and Intention

Today I am grateful for:
- Balance perception of service to self = service to others
- Look in all areas of life

Today's Flip It:
- Balance perceived negative action/inaction until benefits = drawbacks
- Balance perceived positive action/inaction until drawbacks = benefits

My highest priority actions for tomorrow:

MAY 7

He who thanks but with the lips thanks but in part; the full, the true Thanksgiving comes from the heart. — J. A. Shedd

Daily Gratitude and Intention

Today I am grateful for:
- Balance perception of service to self = service to others
- Look in all areas of life

Today's Flip It:
- Balance perceived negative action/inaction until benefits = drawbacks
- Balance perceived positive action/inaction until drawbacks = benefits

My highest priority actions for tomorrow:

Fail to Plan = Plan to Fail.

MAY 8

Daily Gratitude and Intention

Today I am grateful for:
- Balance perception of service to self = service to others
- Look in all areas of life

Today's Flip It:
- Balance perceived negative action/inaction until benefits = drawbacks
- Balance perceived positive action/inaction until drawbacks = benefits

My highest priority actions for tomorrow:

MAY 9

How would your life be different if...you began each day by thanking someone who has helped you? Let today be the day...You make it a point to show your gratitude to others. Send a letter or card, make a call, send a text or email, tell them in person...do whatever you have to do to let them know you appreciate them. — Steve Maraboli

Daily Gratitude and Intention

Today I am grateful for:
- Balance perception of service to self = service to others
- Look in all areas of life

Today's Flip It:
- Balance perceived negative action/inaction until benefits = drawbacks
- Balance perceived positive action/inaction until drawbacks = benefits

My highest priority actions for tomorrow:

There is always the exact opposite positive in any perceived negative behaviour occuring at the exact same moment. Practice finding it in little moments and it will help you balance the bigger challenges faster.
— *Optimum Thinking*

MAY 10

Daily Gratitude and Intention

Today I am grateful for:
- Balance perception of service to self = service to others
- Look in all areas of life

Today's Flip It:
- Balance perceived negative action/inaction until benefits = drawbacks
- Balance perceived positive action/inaction until drawbacks = benefits

My highest priority actions for tomorrow:

MAY 11

I am so grateful for gratitude, a magical magnet. A natural expression of a loving heart, The power of gratitude recharges our souls.
— Katherine Scherer and Eileen Bodoh

Daily Gratitude and Intention

Today I am grateful for:
- Balance perception of service to self = service to others
- Look in all areas of life

....
....
....
....
....
....
....
....
....
....
....

Today's Flip It:
- Balance perceived negative action/inaction until benefits = drawbacks
- Balance perceived positive action/inaction until drawbacks = benefits

....
....
....
....
....

My highest priority actions for tomorrow:
....
....
....
....

No one can make you feel anything. Owning and understanding this is fundamental to mastering your emotions. — Optimum Thinking

MAY 12

Daily Gratitude and Intention

Today I am grateful for:
- Balance perception of service to self = service to others
- Look in all areas of life

Today's Flip It:
- Balance perceived negative action/inaction until benefits = drawbacks
- Balance perceived positive action/inaction until drawbacks = benefits

My highest priority actions for tomorrow:

MAY 13

I am grateful for what I am and have. My thanksgiving is perpetual... O how I laugh when I think of my vague indefinite riches. No run on my bank can drain it for my wealth is not possession but enjoyment.
— Henry David Thoreau

Daily Gratitude and Intention

Today I am grateful for:
- Balance perception of service to self = service to others
- Look in all areas of life

Today's Flip It:
- Balance perceived negative action/inaction until benefits = drawbacks
- Balance perceived positive action/inaction until drawbacks = benefits

My highest priority actions for tomorrow:

We are all Meaning Making Machines. We create our emotions with the meanings we make about what we perceive to have happened.
— Optimum Thinking

MAY 14

Daily Gratitude and Intention

Today I am grateful for:
- Balance perception of service to self = service to others
- Look in all areas of life

Today's Flip It:
- Balance perceived negative action/inaction until benefits = drawbacks
- Balance perceived positive action/inaction until drawbacks = benefits

My highest priority actions for tomorrow:

MAY 15

I awoke this morning with devout thanksgiving for my friends, the old and the new.
— Ralph Waldo Emerson

Daily Gratitude and Intention

Today I am grateful for:
- Balance perception of service to self = service to others
- Look in all areas of life

Today's Flip It:
- Balance perceived negative action/inaction until benefits = drawbacks
- Balance perceived positive action/inaction until drawbacks = benefits

My highest priority actions for tomorrow:

Every action or inaction we choose is a strategy to get what we want. — Optimum Thinking

MAY 16

Daily Gratitude and Intention

Today I am grateful for:
- Balance perception of service to self = service to others
- Look in all areas of life

Today's Flip It:
- Balance perceived negative action/inaction until benefits = drawbacks
- Balance perceived positive action/inaction until drawbacks = benefits

My highest priority actions for tomorrow:

MAY 17

I cannot tell you how to be rich. But I can tell you how to feel rich, which is far better, let me tell you first hand, than being rich. Be grateful. It is the only totally reliable get rich quick scheme.
— Ben Stein

Daily Gratitude and Intention

Today I am grateful for:
- Balance perception of service to self = service to others
- Look in all areas of life

Today's Flip It:
- Balance perceived negative action/inaction until benefits = drawbacks
- Balance perceived positive action/inaction until drawbacks = benefits

My highest priority actions for tomorrow:

Research has shown that we distort our memories by up to 50% based on how we filter an event. We all believe we are more right than other people when we recall an event ... that is why often agreeing on what actually happened can be a slippery eel to catch. — Optimum Thinking

MAY 18

Daily Gratitude and Intention

Today I am grateful for:
- Balance perception of service to self = service to others
- Look in all areas of life

Today's Flip It:
- Balance perceived negative action/inaction until benefits = drawbacks
- Balance perceived positive action/inaction until drawbacks = benefits

My highest priority actions for tomorrow:

MAY 19

I had the blues because I had no shoes until upon the street, I met a man who had no feet.
— Author Unknown

Daily Gratitude and Intention

Today I am grateful for:
- Balance perception of service to self = service to others
- Look in all areas of life

....
....
....
....
....
....
....
....
....
....
....
....

Today's Flip It:
- Balance perceived negative action/inaction until benefits = drawbacks
- Balance perceived positive action/inaction until drawbacks = benefits

....
....
....
....
....

My highest priority actions for tomorrow:
....
....
....
....

> There is no such thing as "good" people and "bad" people. It is more empowering to see everyone as an "Agent of the Universe" with a hierarchy of individual life priorities (HILP) trying to get what they want.
> — Optimum Thinking

MAY 20

Daily Gratitude and Intention

Today I am grateful for:
- Balance perception of service to self = service to others
- Look in all areas of life

Today's Flip It:
- Balance perceived negative action/inaction until benefits = drawbacks
- Balance perceived positive action/inaction until drawbacks = benefits

My highest priority actions for tomorrow:

MAY 21

I have found that it is not enough for me to be thankful. I have a desire to do something in return. To do thanks. To give thanks. Give things. Give thoughts. Give love. So gratitude becomes the gift, creating a cycle of giving and receiving, the endless waterfall. — Elizabeth Bartlett

Daily Gratitude and Intention

Today I am grateful for:
- Balance perception of service to self = service to others
- Look in all areas of life

Today's Flip It:
- Balance perceived negative action/inaction until benefits = drawbacks
- Balance perceived positive action/inaction until drawbacks = benefits

My highest priority actions for tomorrow:

We all possess every action and inaction we list on our polarized "good person" and "bad person" list and we choose to use whatever we believe will get us the best result in the moment. — *Optimum Thinking*

MAY 22

Daily Gratitude and Intention

Today I am grateful for:
- Balance perception of service to self = service to others
- Look in all areas of life

Today's Flip It:
- Balance perceived negative action/inaction until benefits = drawbacks
- Balance perceived positive action/inaction until drawbacks = benefits

My highest priority actions for tomorrow:

MAY 23

I have learned that in every circumstance that comes my way, I can choose to respond in one of two ways: I can whine or I can worship! And I can't worship without giving thanks. It just isn't possible.
— Nancy Leigh DeMoss

Daily Gratitude and Intention

Today I am grateful for:
- Balance perception of service to self = service to others
- Look in all areas of life

Today's Flip It:
- Balance perceived negative action/inaction until benefits = drawbacks
- Balance perceived positive action/inaction until drawbacks = benefits

My highest priority actions for tomorrow:

Overdogs attract humbling circumstances. If you feel yourself puffing up and getting proud, ask yourself the right questions to bring you back to balance before external forces do. — Optimum Thinking

MAY 24

Daily Gratitude and Intention

Today I am grateful for:
- Balance perception of service to self = service to others
- Look in all areas of life

Today's Flip It:
- Balance perceived negative action/inaction until benefits = drawbacks
- Balance perceived positive action/inaction until drawbacks = benefits

My highest priority actions for tomorrow:

MAY 25

I try hard to hold fast to the truth that a full and thankful heart cannot entertain great conceits. When brimming with gratitude, one's heartbeat must surely result in outgoing love, the finest emotion we can ever know. — Bill W

Daily Gratitude and Intention

Today I am grateful for:
- Balance perception of service to self = service to others
- Look in all areas of life

Today's Flip It:
- Balance perceived negative action/inaction until benefits = drawbacks
- Balance perceived positive action/inaction until drawbacks = benefits

My highest priority actions for tomorrow:

We each use whatever action or inaction we believe will give us the most benefit at the time... so does everyone else. — Optimum Thinking

MAY 26

Daily Gratitude and Intention

Today I am grateful for:
- Balance perception of service to self = service to others
- Look in all areas of life

Today's Flip It:
- Balance perceived negative action/inaction until benefits = drawbacks
- Balance perceived positive action/inaction until drawbacks = benefits

My highest priority actions for tomorrow:

MAY 27

There is nothing in a caterpillar that tells you it is going to be a butterfly. — Buckminster Fuller

Daily Gratitude and Intention

Today I am grateful for:
- Balance perception of service to self = service to others
- Look in all areas of life

Today's Flip It:
- Balance perceived negative action/inaction until benefits = drawbacks
- Balance perceived positive action/inaction until drawbacks = benefits

My highest priority actions for tomorrow:

What if you chose the perfect parents to both support and challenge you to become perfectly you and there were no mistakes? — Optimum Thinking

MAY 28

Daily Gratitude and Intention

Today I am grateful for:
- Balance perception of service to self = service to others
- Look in all areas of life

Today's Flip It:
- Balance perceived negative action/inaction until benefits = drawbacks
- Balance perceived positive action/inaction until drawbacks = benefits

My highest priority actions for tomorrow:

MAY 29

I would maintain that thanks are the highest form of thought; and that gratitude is happiness doubled by wonder. — G.K. Chesterton

Daily Gratitude and Intention

Today I am grateful for:
- Balance perception of service to self = service to others
- Look in all areas of life

Today's Flip It:
- Balance perceived negative action/inaction until benefits = drawbacks
- Balance perceived positive action/inaction until drawbacks = benefits

My highest priority actions for tomorrow:

Practice your Optimum Thinking daily and harness the power of positive and negative thinking. — Optimum Thinking

MAY 30

Daily Gratitude and Intention

Today I am grateful for:
- Balance perception of service to self = service to others
- Look in all areas of life

Today's Flip It:
- Balance perceived negative action/inaction until benefits = drawbacks
- Balance perceived positive action/inaction until drawbacks = benefits

My highest priority actions for tomorrow:

MAY 31

Energy and vitality are infinite when you recognize and appreciate their source: a heart filled with gratitude. — John Demartini

Daily Gratitude and Intention

Today I am grateful for:
- Balance perception of service to self = service to others
- Look in all areas of life

Today's Flip It:
- Balance perceived negative action/inaction until benefits = drawbacks
- Balance perceived positive action/inaction until drawbacks = benefits

My highest priority actions for tomorrow:

JUNE

Monthly Intention Plan

Write the top priorities you intend to focus on in each area of your life during this month.

SPIRITUAL / MISSION / SELF-ACTUALIZATION

MENTAL / EDUCATION

VOCATION / CAREER

FINANCIAL WEALTH / SAVING & INVESTING

FAMILY / RELATIONSHIP

SOCIAL / FRIENDS

HEALTH & PHYSICAL APPEARANCE

JUN 1

The world is so exquisite with so much love and moral depth, that there is no reason to deceive ourselves with pretty stories for which there's little good evidence. Far better it seems to me, in our vulnerability, is to look death in the eye and to be grateful every day for the brief but magnificent opportunity that life provides. — Carl Sagan

Daily Gratitude and Intention

Today I am grateful for:
- Balance perception of service to self = service to others
- Look in all areas of life

Today's Flip It:
- Balance perceived negative action/inaction until benefits = drawbacks
- Balance perceived positive action/inaction until drawbacks = benefits

My highest priority actions for tomorrow:

Competitors compete with each other. Champions compete with themselves. — Optimum Thinking

JUN 2

Daily Gratitude and Intention

Today I am grateful for:
- Balance perception of service to self = service to others
- Look in all areas of life

Today's Flip It:
- Balance perceived negative action/inaction until benefits = drawbacks
- Balance perceived positive action/inaction until drawbacks = benefits

My highest priority actions for tomorrow:

JUN 3

Never be afraid or hesitant to step off the accepted path and head off in your own direction, if your heart tells you that it's the right way for you. Always believe that you will ultimately succeed at whatever you do, and never forget the value of persistence, discipline, and determination. You are meant to be whatever you dream of becoming.
— Edmund O'Neill

Daily Gratitude and Intention

Today I am grateful for:
- Balance perception of service to self = service to others
- Look in all areas of life

Today's Flip It:
- Balance perceived negative action/inaction until benefits = drawbacks
- Balance perceived positive action/inaction until drawbacks = benefits

My highest priority actions for tomorrow:

If you are doing a 'pity party' take the time to list what you are grateful for in all areas of your life. Keep this list, re-read it and add to it any time in the future you find yourself slipping into a negative state. There is always fair exchange. — Optimum Thinking

JUN 4

Daily Gratitude and Intention

Today I am grateful for:
- Balance perception of service to self = service to others
- Look in all areas of life

Today's Flip It:
- Balance perceived negative action/inaction until benefits = drawbacks
- Balance perceived positive action/inaction until drawbacks = benefits

My highest priority actions for tomorrow:

JUN 5

If people offer their help or wisdom as you go through life, accept it gratefully. You can learn much from those who have gone before you. — Edmund O'Neill

Daily Gratitude and Intention

Today I am grateful for:
- Balance perception of service to self = service to others
- Look in all areas of life

Today's Flip It:
- Balance perceived negative action/inaction until benefits = drawbacks
- Balance perceived positive action/inaction until drawbacks = benefits

My highest priority actions for tomorrow:

Infatuation keeps us stuck in fantasy and reduces our ability to live in and appreciate the present and the gifts life has already given us. — Optimum Thinking

JUN 6

Daily Gratitude and Intention

Today I am grateful for:
- Balance perception of service to self = service to others
- Look in all areas of life

Today's Flip It:
- Balance perceived negative action/inaction until benefits = drawbacks
- Balance perceived positive action/inaction until drawbacks = benefits

My highest priority actions for tomorrow:

JUN 7

I don't have to chase extraordinary moments to find happiness – it's right in front of me if I'm paying attention and practicing gratitude. — Brene Brown

Daily Gratitude and Intention

Today I am grateful for:
- Balance perception of service to self = service to others
- Look in all areas of life

Today's Flip It:
- Balance perceived negative action/inaction until benefits = drawbacks
- Balance perceived positive action/inaction until drawbacks = benefits

My highest priority actions for tomorrow:

Find the gifts and lessons in every challenge you perceive. Overcoming the challenges is what births your leadership and develops your problem-solving and resillience. — Optimum Thinking

JUN 8

Daily Gratitude and Intention

Today I am grateful for:
- Balance perception of service to self = service to others
- Look in all areas of life

Today's Flip It:
- Balance perceived negative action/inaction until benefits = drawbacks
- Balance perceived positive action/inaction until drawbacks = benefits

My highest priority actions for tomorrow:

JUN 9

If you concentrate on finding whatever is good in every situation, you will discover that your life will suddenly be filled with gratitude, a feeling that nurtures the soul.
— Rabbi Harold Kushner

Daily Gratitude and Intention

Today I am grateful for:
- Balance perception of service to self = service to others
- Look in all areas of life

Today's Flip It:
- Balance perceived negative action/inaction until benefits = drawbacks
- Balance perceived positive action/inaction until drawbacks = benefits

My highest priority actions for tomorrow:

The only constant is transformation. Take the time to find equal benefits and drawbacks in any transformation you perceive in your life as they occur. This will help you stay balanced, grateful and vital. — Optimum Thinking

JUN 10

Daily Gratitude and Intention

Today I am grateful for:
- Balance perception of service to self = service to others
- Look in all areas of life

Today's Flip It:
- Balance perceived negative action/inaction until benefits = drawbacks
- Balance perceived positive action/inaction until drawbacks = benefits

My highest priority actions for tomorrow:

JUN 11

If you count all your assets, you always show a profit.
— Robert Quillen

Daily Gratitude and Intention

Today I am grateful for:
- Balance perception of service to self = service to others
- Look in all areas of life

Today's Flip It:
- Balance perceived negative action/inaction until benefits = drawbacks
- Balance perceived positive action/inaction until drawbacks = benefits

My highest priority actions for tomorrow:

Separate perceived negative actions/inactions from the person. The action is no more than a tool the person is using to try to get what they want. Choose to perceive the balance in the action and still love the person.
— Optimum Thinking

JUN 12

Daily Gratitude and Intention

Today I am grateful for:
- Balance perception of service to self = service to others
- Look in all areas of life

Today's Flip It:
- Balance perceived negative action/inaction until benefits = drawbacks
- Balance perceived positive action/inaction until drawbacks = benefits

My highest priority actions for tomorrow:

JUN 13

If you have true gratitude, it will express itself automatically. It will be visible in your eyes, around your being, in your aur. — Sri Chinmoy

Daily Gratitude and Intention

Today I am grateful for:
- Balance perception of service to self = service to others
- Look in all areas of life

Today's Flip It:
- Balance perceived negative action/inaction until benefits = drawbacks
- Balance perceived positive action/inaction until drawbacks = benefits

My highest priority actions for tomorrow:

How would you treat the environment when you have certainty that you will reincarnate repeatedly and never know who you will return as? — Optimum Thinking

JUN 14

Daily Gratitude and Intention

Today I am grateful for:
- Balance perception of service to self = service to others
- Look in all areas of life

Today's Flip It:
- Balance perceived negative action/inaction until benefits = drawbacks
- Balance perceived positive action/inaction until drawbacks = benefits

My highest priority actions for tomorrow:

JUN 15

If you want to turn your life around, try thankfulness. It will change your life mightily. — Gerald Good

Daily Gratitude and Intention

Today I am grateful for:
- Balance perception of service to self = service to others
- Look in all areas of life

Today's Flip It:
- Balance perceived negative action/inaction until benefits = drawbacks
- Balance perceived positive action/inaction until drawbacks = benefits

My highest priority actions for tomorrow:

How would you treat other people and races when you have certainty that you will reincarnate repeatedly and never know who you will return as? — Optimum Thinking

JUN 16

Daily Gratitude and Intention

Today I am grateful for:
- Balance perception of service to self = service to others
- Look in all areas of life

Today's Flip It:
- Balance perceived negative action/inaction until benefits = drawbacks
- Balance perceived positive action/inaction until drawbacks = benefits

My highest priority actions for tomorrow:

JUN 17

In all things, give thanks. — Holy Bible

Daily Gratitude and Intention

Today I am grateful for:
- Balance perception of service to self = service to others
- Look in all areas of life

Today's Flip It:
- Balance perceived negative action/inaction until benefits = drawbacks
- Balance perceived positive action/inaction until drawbacks = benefits

My highest priority actions for tomorrow:

We are all Double Agents of the Universe both supporting and challenging each other to transform and achieve our Optimum Life Missions. — Optimum Thinking

JUN 18

Daily Gratitude and Intention

Today I am grateful for:
- Balance perception of service to self = service to others
- Look in all areas of life

Today's Flip It:
- Balance perceived negative action/inaction until benefits = drawbacks
- Balance perceived positive action/inaction until drawbacks = benefits

My highest priority actions for tomorrow:

JUN 19

When we are no longer able to change a situation, we are challenged to change ourselves. — Viktor Frankl

Daily Gratitude and Intention

Today I am grateful for:
- Balance perception of service to self = service to others
- Look in all areas of life

Today's Flip It:
- Balance perceived negative action/inaction until benefits = drawbacks
- Balance perceived positive action/inaction until drawbacks = benefits

My highest priority actions for tomorrow:

In life one has two choices; to wait for that special day – or to celebrate each day as special by finding and expressing gratitude. — Optimum Thinking

JUN 20

Daily Gratitude and Intention

Today I am grateful for:
- Balance perception of service to self = service to others
- Look in all areas of life

Today's Flip It:
- Balance perceived negative action/inaction until benefits = drawbacks
- Balance perceived positive action/inaction until drawbacks = benefits

My highest priority actions for tomorrow:

JUN 21

In normal life we hardly realize how much more we receive than we give, and life cannot be rich without such gratitude. It is so easy to overestimate the importance of our own achievements compared with what we owe to the help of others. — Dietrich Bonhoeffer

Daily Gratitude and Intention

Today I am grateful for:
- Balance perception of service to self = service to others
- Look in all areas of life

Today's Flip It:
- Balance perceived negative action/inaction until benefits = drawbacks
- Balance perceived positive action/inaction until drawbacks = benefits

My highest priority actions for tomorrow:

Completing your annual and monthly planning is a powerful way to assess what is really important to you. You will have real evidence of where you actually have choosen to invest your resources and help you clarify what you want moving forward.
— Optimum Thinking

JUN 22

Daily Gratitude and Intention

Today I am grateful for:
- Balance perception of service to self = service to others
- Look in all areas of life

Today's Flip It:
- Balance perceived negative action/inaction until benefits = drawbacks
- Balance perceived positive action/inaction until drawbacks = benefits

My highest priority actions for tomorrow:

JUN 23

Inspiration is everywhere. If you're ready to appreciate it, an ant can be one of the wonders of the world.
— Anonymous

Daily Gratitude and Intention

Today I am grateful for:
- Balance perception of service to self = service to others
- Look in all areas of life

Today's Flip It:
- Balance perceived negative action/inaction until benefits = drawbacks
- Balance perceived positive action/inaction until drawbacks = benefits

My highest priority actions for tomorrow:

People who act like an Underdog and play small will attact challenging circumstances to kick them back into action and growth. — Optimum Thinking.

JUN 24

Daily Gratitude and Intention

Today I am grateful for:
- Balance perception of service to self = service to others
- Look in all areas of life

Today's Flip It:
- Balance perceived negative action/inaction until benefits = drawbacks
- Balance perceived positive action/inaction until drawbacks = benefits

My highest priority actions for tomorrow:

JUN 25

It doesn't matter what you did or where you were... it matters where you are and what you're doing. Get out there! Sing the song in your heart and NEVER let anyone shut you up!! — Steve Maraboli

Daily Gratitude and Intention

Today I am grateful for:
- Balance perception of service to self = service to others
- Look in all areas of life

Today's Flip It:
- Balance perceived negative action/inaction until benefits = drawbacks
- Balance perceived positive action/inaction until drawbacks = benefits

My highest priority actions for tomorrow:

> *You program yourself with the words you use. Watch out for "victim language". When you blame others for what you have attracted into your life you are giving your power away. If you have attracted challenges there are benefits in it for you, if you take the time to think hard and find them.*
> — *Optimum Thinking*

JUN 26

Daily Gratitude and Intention

Today I am grateful for:
- Balance perception of service to self = service to others
- Look in all areas of life

Today's Flip It:
- Balance perceived negative action/inaction until benefits = drawbacks
- Balance perceived positive action/inaction until drawbacks = benefits

My highest priority actions for tomorrow:

JUN 27

Ingratitude produces pride while gratitude produces humility.
— Orrin Woodward

Daily Gratitude and Intention

Today I am grateful for:
- Balance perception of service to self = service to others
- Look in all areas of life

Today's Flip It:
- Balance perceived negative action/inaction until benefits = drawbacks
- Balance perceived positive action/inaction until drawbacks = benefits

My highest priority actions for tomorrow:

If you seek a life that is happy all of the time, you are setting yourself up for failure. Instead seek a fulfilled like where you embrace both challenge and support to get what you want. — Optimum Thinking

JUN 28

Daily Gratitude and Intention

Today I am grateful for:
- Balance perception of service to self = service to others
- Look in all areas of life

Today's Flip It:
- Balance perceived negative action/inaction until benefits = drawbacks
- Balance perceived positive action/inaction until drawbacks = benefits

My highest priority actions for tomorrow:

JUN 29

Joy is the simplest expression of gratitude.
— *Optimum Thinking*

Daily Gratitude and Intention

Today I am grateful for:
- Balance perception of service to self = service to others
- Look in all areas of life

Today's Flip It:
- Balance perceived negative action/inaction until benefits = drawbacks
- Balance perceived positive action/inaction until drawbacks = benefits

My highest priority actions for tomorrow:

There is only one person who can give you "self-esteem". If you are beating yourself up, find where you know you have skills and abilities that are above other people until you perceive you are equal to others and perfectly, uniquely you.
— Optimum Thinking

JUN 30

Daily Gratitude and Intention

Today I am grateful for:
- Balance perception of service to self = service to others
- Look in all areas of life

Today's Flip It:
- Balance perceived negative action/inaction until benefits = drawbacks
- Balance perceived positive action/inaction until drawbacks = benefits

My highest priority actions for tomorrow:

JULY

Monthly Intention Plan

Write the top priorities you intend to focus on in each area of your life during this month.

SPIRITUAL / MISSION / SELF-ACTUALIZATION

MENTAL / EDUCATION

VOCATION / CAREER

FINANCIAL WEALTH / SAVING & INVESTING

FAMILY / RELATIONSHIP

SOCIAL / FRIENDS

HEALTH & PHYSICAL APPEARANCE

JUL 1

Just as millions of snowflakes pile up to create a blanket of snow, the thank you's we say pile up and fall gently upon one another until, in our hearts and minds, we are adrift in gratitude.
— Daphne Rose Kingman

Daily Gratitude and Intention

Today I am grateful for:
- Balance perception of service to self = service to others
- Look in all areas of life

Today's Flip It:
- Balance perceived negative action/inaction until benefits = drawbacks
- Balance perceived positive action/inaction until drawbacks = benefits

My highest priority actions for tomorrow:

There is a divine intelligence that is beyond our comprehesion that is running this show we call life. The wisdom of this intelligence has set us up to strive to achieve, learn and grow. When you are wallowing in a 'pity party' you have forgotten your purpose and what it will take to achieve it. Set goals and get your hands back on the steering wheel of your life!
— *Optimum Thinking*

JUL 2

Daily Gratitude and Intention

Today I am grateful for:
- Balance perception of service to self = service to others
- Look in all areas of life

Today's Flip It:
- Balance perceived negative action/inaction until benefits = drawbacks
- Balance perceived positive action/inaction until drawbacks = benefits

My highest priority actions for tomorrow:

JUL 3

Let us be grateful to those people who help us express happiness; they are the thoughtful gardeners who help our hearts bloom. — Optimum Thinking

Daily Gratitude and Intention

Today I am grateful for:
- Balance perception of service to self = service to others
- Look in all areas of life

Today's Flip It:
- Balance perceived negative action/inaction until benefits = drawbacks
- Balance perceived positive action/inaction until drawbacks = benefits

My highest priority actions for tomorrow:

When a parent sets a boundary for their child, it is because they love them enough to do something the child may perceive as 'bad'. Understanding boundaries is critical for us to live as a family and society. — Optimum Thinking

JUL 4

Daily Gratitude and Intention

Today I am grateful for:
- Balance perception of service to self = service to others
- Look in all areas of life

Today's Flip It:
- Balance perceived negative action/inaction until benefits = drawbacks
- Balance perceived positive action/inaction until drawbacks = benefits

My highest priority actions for tomorrow:

JUL 5

Let us remember that, as much has been given us, much will be expected from us, and that true homage comes from the heart as well as from the lips, and shows itself in deeds.
— Theodore Roosevelt

Daily Gratitude and Intention

Today I am grateful for:
- Balance perception of service to self = service to others
- Look in all areas of life

Today's Flip It:
- Balance perceived negative action/inaction until benefits = drawbacks
- Balance perceived positive action/inaction until drawbacks = benefits

My highest priority actions for tomorrow:

If you are not achieving a goal, assess why you haven't. If it is too big, break it down into smaller steps. If it is not important enough to you, delete it. Live the life you consciously choose! — Optimum Thinking

JUL 6

Daily Gratitude and Intention

Today I am grateful for:
- Balance perception of service to self = service to others
- Look in all areas of life

Today's Flip It:
- Balance perceived negative action/inaction until benefits = drawbacks
- Balance perceived positive action/inaction until drawbacks = benefits

My highest priority actions for tomorrow:

JUL 7

Let us rise up and be thankful, for if we didn't learn a lot today, at least we learned a little, and if we didn't learn a little, at least we didn't get sick, and if we got sick, at least we didn't die; so, let us all be thankful. — Buddha

Daily Gratitude and Intention

Today I am grateful for:
- Balance perception of service to self = service to others
- Look in all areas of life

Today's Flip It:
- Balance perceived negative action/inaction until benefits = drawbacks
- Balance perceived positive action/inaction until drawbacks = benefits

My highest priority actions for tomorrow:

JUL 8

Being able to live a one-sided "happy" life is a delusion. Practise the art of appreciating the value of overcoming challenges in your life – the bigger the challenge the more you grow. Being grateful for both sides of life means you are truly living a fulfilling life. — Optimum Thinking

Daily Gratitude and Intention

Today I am grateful for:
- Balance perception of service to self = service to others
- Look in all areas of life

Today's Flip It:
- Balance perceived negative action/inaction until benefits = drawbacks
- Balance perceived positive action/inaction until drawbacks = benefits

My highest priority actions for tomorrow:

JUL 9

Live your life so that the fear of death can never enter your heart. When you arise in the morning, give thanks for the morning light. Give thanks for your life and strength. Give thanks for your food and for the joy of living. And if perchance you see no reason for giving thanks, rest assured the fault is in yourself. Chief Tecumseh, — Shawnee Indian Chief

Daily Gratitude and Intention

Today I am grateful for:
- Balance perception of service to self = service to others
- Look in all areas of life

Today's Flip It:
- Balance perceived negative action/inaction until benefits = drawbacks
- Balance perceived positive action/inaction until drawbacks = benefits

My highest priority actions for tomorrow:

You live your Optimum Life when you consciously choose what you want, plan how to get it and learn to clear emotional charge that gets in the way. — Optimum Thinking

JUL 10

Daily Gratitude and Intention

Today I am grateful for:
- Balance perception of service to self = service to others
- Look in all areas of life

Today's Flip It:
- Balance perceived negative action/inaction until benefits = drawbacks
- Balance perceived positive action/inaction until drawbacks = benefits

My highest priority actions for tomorrow:

JUL 11

> We need to accept that we won't always make the right decisions, that we'll screw up royally sometimes – understanding that failure is not the opposite of success, it's part of success. — Arianna Huffington

Daily Gratitude and Intention

Today I am grateful for:
- Balance perception of service to self = service to others
- Look in all areas of life

Today's Flip It:
- Balance perceived negative action/inaction until benefits = drawbacks
- Balance perceived positive action/inaction until drawbacks = benefits

My highest priority actions for tomorrow:

If you perceive something is "too good to be true" then it is time to do some work and find all of the drawbacks to it until you can see it has both sides equally. If you don't, you will be gullible and likely to be overpowered in some way.
— Optimum Thinking

JUL 12

Daily Gratitude and Intention

Today I am grateful for:
- Balance perception of service to self = service to others
- Look in all areas of life

Today's Flip It:
- Balance perceived negative action/inaction until benefits = drawbacks
- Balance perceived positive action/inaction until drawbacks = benefits

My highest priority actions for tomorrow:

JUL 13

Make it a habit to tell people thank you. To express your appreciation, sincerely and without the expectation of anything in return. Truly appreciate those around you, and you'll soon find many others around you. Truly appreciate life, and you'll find that you have more of it. — Ralph Marston

Daily Gratitude and Intention

Today I am grateful for:
- Balance perception of service to self = service to others
- Look in all areas of life

Today's Flip It:
- Balance perceived negative action/inaction until benefits = drawbacks
- Balance perceived positive action/inaction until drawbacks = benefits

My highest priority actions for tomorrow:

Life wasn't meant to be easy. It is meant to be fulfilling. You will never feel fulfilled if you haven't set yourself challenges and overcome them! — *Optimum Thinking*

JUL 14

Daily Gratitude and Intention

Today I am grateful for:
- Balance perception of service to self = service to others
- Look in all areas of life

Today's Flip It:
- Balance perceived negative action/inaction until benefits = drawbacks
- Balance perceived positive action/inaction until drawbacks = benefits

My highest priority actions for tomorrow:

JUL 15

Many people who order their lives rightly in all other ways are kept in poverty by their lack of gratitude.
— Wallace Wattles

Daily Gratitude and Intention

Today I am grateful for:
- Balance perception of service to self = service to others
- Look in all areas of life

Today's Flip It:
- Balance perceived negative action/inaction until benefits = drawbacks
- Balance perceived positive action/inaction until drawbacks = benefits

My highest priority actions for tomorrow:

If you perceive you had a boring day today, think about what you may have missed out on by not managing your emotional state and intention. — Optimum Thinking

JUL 16

Daily Gratitude and Intention

Today I am grateful for:
- Balance perception of service to self = service to others
- Look in all areas of life

Today's Flip It:
- Balance perceived negative action/inaction until benefits = drawbacks
- Balance perceived positive action/inaction until drawbacks = benefits

My highest priority actions for tomorrow:

JUL 17

Most of us forget to take time for wonder, praise and gratitude until it is almost too late. Gratitude is a many-colored quality, reaching in all directions. It goes out for small things and for large. — Faith Baldwin

Daily Gratitude and Intention

Today I am grateful for:
- Balance perception of service to self = service to others
- Look in all areas of life

Today's Flip It:
- Balance perceived negative action/inaction until benefits = drawbacks
- Balance perceived positive action/inaction until drawbacks = benefits

My highest priority actions for tomorrow:

Optimum Thinking skills take work. The more you put in, the more you accelerate your achievements and relationships. — Optimum Thinking.

JUL 18

Daily Gratitude and Intention

Today I am grateful for:
- Balance perception of service to self = service to others
- Look in all areas of life

Today's Flip It:
- Balance perceived negative action/inaction until benefits = drawbacks
- Balance perceived positive action/inaction until drawbacks = benefits

My highest priority actions for tomorrow:

JUL 19

It took me a long time to realize we are not meant to be perfect; we're meant to be whole. — Jane Fonda

Daily Gratitude and Intention

Today I am grateful for:
- Balance perception of service to self = service to others
- Look in all areas of life

Today's Flip It:
- Balance perceived negative action/inaction until benefits = drawbacks
- Balance perceived positive action/inaction until drawbacks = benefits

My highest priority actions for tomorrow:

Plan your Optimum Life and live your love. Don't blame other people for not getting what you want. They are all busy working on getting what they want! — Optimum Thinking

JUL 20

Daily Gratitude and Intention

Today I am grateful for:
- Balance perception of service to self = service to others
- Look in all areas of life

Today's Flip It:
- Balance perceived negative action/inaction until benefits = drawbacks
- Balance perceived positive action/inaction until drawbacks = benefits

My highest priority actions for tomorrow:

JUL 21

No one who achieves success does so without acknowledging the help of others. The wise and confident acknowledge this help with gratitude.
— Alfred North Whitehead

Daily Gratitude and Intention

Today I am grateful for:
- Balance perception of service to self = service to others
- Look in all areas of life

Today's Flip It:
- Balance perceived negative action/inaction until benefits = drawbacks
- Balance perceived positive action/inaction until drawbacks = benefits

My highest priority actions for tomorrow:

Our language is full of polarization that encourages emotional reactions. Try using hyphens to find more balanced language e.g. humbly-empowered.
— Optimum Thinking

JUL 22

Daily Gratitude and Intention

Today I am grateful for:
- Balance perception of service to self = service to others
- Look in all areas of life

Today's Flip It:
- Balance perceived negative action/inaction until benefits = drawbacks
- Balance perceived positive action/inaction until drawbacks = benefits

My highest priority actions for tomorrow:

JUL 23

Not what we say about our blessings, but how we use them, is the true measure of our thanksgiving.
— W.T. Purkiser

Daily Gratitude and Intention

Today I am grateful for:
- Balance perception of service to self = service to others
- Look in all areas of life

Today's Flip It:
- Balance perceived negative action/inaction until benefits = drawbacks
- Balance perceived positive action/inaction until drawbacks = benefits

My highest priority actions for tomorrow:

Gratitude, joy, inspiration and enthusiasm are the emotional states of an open heart. — Optimum Thinking

JUL 24

Daily Gratitude and Intention

Today I am grateful for:
- Balance perception of service to self = service to others
- Look in all areas of life

Today's Flip It:
- Balance perceived negative action/inaction until benefits = drawbacks
- Balance perceived positive action/inaction until drawbacks = benefits

My highest priority actions for tomorrow:

JUL 25

O Lord that lends me life, Lend me a heart replete with thankfulness! — William Shakespeare

Daily Gratitude and Intention

Today I am grateful for:
- Balance perception of service to self = service to others
- Look in all areas of life

Today's Flip It:
- Balance perceived negative action/inaction until benefits = drawbacks
- Balance perceived positive action/inaction until drawbacks = benefits

My highest priority actions for tomorrow:

Overdogs have care-less relationships. Underdogs are too care-ful in relationships and feel like they are treading on egg shells. Optimum dogs have caring relationships. They see their partner as equal and both challenge and support them to grow and achieve. — Optimum Thinking

JUL 26

Daily Gratitude and Intention

Today I am grateful for:
- Balance perception of service to self = service to others
- Look in all areas of life

Today's Flip It:
- Balance perceived negative action/inaction until benefits = drawbacks
- Balance perceived positive action/inaction until drawbacks = benefits

My highest priority actions for tomorrow:

JUL 27

One looks back with appreciation to the brilliant teachers, but with gratitude to those who touched our human feelings. The curriculum is so much necessary raw material, but warmth is the vital element for the growing plant and for the soul of the child. — Carl Jung

Daily Gratitude and Intention

Today I am grateful for:
- Balance perception of service to self = service to others
- Look in all areas of life

Today's Flip It:
- Balance perceived negative action/inaction until benefits = drawbacks
- Balance perceived positive action/inaction until drawbacks = benefits

My highest priority actions for tomorrow:

Make a point of expressing you gratitude to someone today. — Optimum Thinking

JUL 28

Daily Gratitude and Intention

Today I am grateful for:
- Balance perception of service to self = service to others
- Look in all areas of life

Today's Flip It:
- Balance perceived negative action/inaction until benefits = drawbacks
- Balance perceived positive action/inaction until drawbacks = benefits

My highest priority actions for tomorrow:

JUL 29

Only a stomach that rarely feels hungry scorns common things. — Horace

Daily Gratitude and Intention

Today I am grateful for:
- Balance perception of service to self = service to others
- Look in all areas of life

Today's Flip It:
- Balance perceived negative action/inaction until benefits = drawbacks
- Balance perceived positive action/inaction until drawbacks = benefits

My highest priority actions for tomorrow:

When you feel angry about something someone did to you, ask yourself how what they did will help you achieve what is important to you until you perceive the benefits are equal to the drawbacks. — Optimum Thinking

JUL 30

Daily Gratitude and Intention

Today I am grateful for:
- Balance perception of service to self = service to others
- Look in all areas of life

Today's Flip It:
- Balance perceived negative action/inaction until benefits = drawbacks
- Balance perceived positive action/inaction until drawbacks = benefits

My highest priority actions for tomorrow:

JUL 31

Piglet noticed that even though he had a Very Small Heart, it could hold a rather large amount of Gratitude.
— A.A. Milne

Daily Gratitude and Intention

Today I am grateful for:
- Balance perception of service to self = service to others
- Look in all areas of life

Today's Flip It:
- Balance perceived negative action/inaction until benefits = drawbacks
- Balance perceived positive action/inaction until drawbacks = benefits

My highest priority actions for tomorrow:

AUGUST

Monthly Intention Plan

Write the top priorities you intend to focus on in each area of your life during this month.

SPIRITUAL / MISSION / SELF-ACTUALIZATION

MENTAL / EDUCATION

VOCATION / CAREER

FINANCIAL WEALTH / SAVING & INVESTING

FAMILY / RELATIONSHIP

SOCIAL / FRIENDS

HEALTH & PHYSICAL APPEARANCE

AUG 1

Praise the bridge that carried you over. — George Colman

Daily Gratitude and Intention

Today I am grateful for:
- Balance perception of service to self = service to others
- Look in all areas of life

Today's Flip It:
- Balance perceived negative action/inaction until benefits = drawbacks
- Balance perceived positive action/inaction until drawbacks = benefits

My highest priority actions for tomorrow:

You are the only person who can inspire you — it is a feeling in your heart. You are in control of your emotional state. What emotional state do you want to create today?
— Optimum Thinking

AUG 2

Daily Gratitude and Intention

Today I am grateful for:
- Balance perception of service to self = service to others
- Look in all areas of life

Today's Flip It:
- Balance perceived negative action/inaction until benefits = drawbacks
- Balance perceived positive action/inaction until drawbacks = benefits

My highest priority actions for tomorrow:

AUG 3

Rather than getting more spoilt with age, as difficulties pile up, epiphanies of gratitude abound. — Alain de Botton

Daily Gratitude and Intention

Today I am grateful for:
- Balance perception of service to self = service to others
- Look in all areas of life

Today's Flip It:
- Balance perceived negative action/inaction until benefits = drawbacks
- Balance perceived positive action/inaction until drawbacks = benefits

My highest priority actions for tomorrow:

When you feel guilty about something you did to someone, ask yourself how what you did helped them achieve what is important to them until you perceive the benefits to them are equal to the drawbacks. — Optimum Thinking

AUG 4

Daily Gratitude and Intention

Today I am grateful for:
- Balance perception of service to self = service to others
- Look in all areas of life

Today's Flip It:
- Balance perceived negative action/inaction until benefits = drawbacks
- Balance perceived positive action/inaction until drawbacks = benefits

My highest priority actions for tomorrow:

AUG 5

Reflect upon your present blessings, of which every man has plenty; not on your past misfortunes, of which all men have some.
— Charles Dickens

Daily Gratitude and Intention

Today I am grateful for:
- Balance perception of service to self = service to others
- Look in all areas of life

Today's Flip It:
- Balance perceived negative action/inaction until benefits = drawbacks
- Balance perceived positive action/inaction until drawbacks = benefits

My highest priority actions for tomorrow:

Optimum Thinking ... when positive thinking just isn't enough. — Optimum Thinking

AUG 6

Daily Gratitude and Intention

Today I am grateful for:
- Balance perception of service to self = service to others
- Look in all areas of life

Today's Flip It:
- Balance perceived negative action/inaction until benefits = drawbacks
- Balance perceived positive action/inaction until drawbacks = benefits

My highest priority actions for tomorrow:

AUG 7

It does not matter how slowly you go as long as you do not stop. — Confucius

Daily Gratitude and Intention

Today I am grateful for:
- Balance perception of service to self = service to others
- Look in all areas of life

....

Today's Flip It:
- Balance perceived negative action/inaction until benefits = drawbacks
- Balance perceived positive action/inaction until drawbacks = benefits

....

My highest priority actions for tomorrow:

....

Life-changing gratitude requires very specific regular attention and intention to become a habit of the mind and soul. — Optimum Thinking

AUG 8

Daily Gratitude and Intention

Today I am grateful for:
- Balance perception of service to self = service to others
- Look in all areas of life

Today's Flip It:
- Balance perceived negative action/inaction until benefits = drawbacks
- Balance perceived positive action/inaction until drawbacks = benefits

My highest priority actions for tomorrow:

AUG 9

So much about living life, to me, is about humility and gratitude. — Katherine Heigl

Daily Gratitude and Intention

Today I am grateful for:
- Balance perception of service to self = service to others
- Look in all areas of life

Today's Flip It:
- Balance perceived negative action/inaction until benefits = drawbacks
- Balance perceived positive action/inaction until drawbacks = benefits

My highest priority actions for tomorrow:

You have programmed yourself with your beliefs. Bring to mind as many as you can and check if they empower or disempower you. — Optimum Thinking

AUG 10

Daily Gratitude and Intention

Today I am grateful for:
- Balance perception of service to self = service to others
- Look in all areas of life

Today's Flip It:
- Balance perceived negative action/inaction until benefits = drawbacks
- Balance perceived positive action/inaction until drawbacks = benefits

My highest priority actions for tomorrow:

AUG 11

Sometimes life knocks you on your ass...get up, get up, get up!!! Happiness is not the absence of problems, it's the ability to deal with them. — Steve Maraboli

Daily Gratitude and Intention

Today I am grateful for:
- Balance perception of service to self = service to others
- Look in all areas of life

Today's Flip It:
- Balance perceived negative action/inaction until benefits = drawbacks
- Balance perceived positive action/inaction until drawbacks = benefits

My highest priority actions for tomorrow:

You change disempowering beliefs by finding new data that supports a more empowering belief until you choose to adopt it. — Optimum Thinking

AUG 12

Daily Gratitude and Intention

Today I am grateful for:
- Balance perception of service to self = service to others
- Look in all areas of life

Today's Flip It:
- Balance perceived negative action/inaction until benefits = drawbacks
- Balance perceived positive action/inaction until drawbacks = benefits

My highest priority actions for tomorrow:

AUG 13

The final forming of a person's character lies in their own hands. — Ann Frank

Daily Gratitude and Intention

Today I am grateful for:
- Balance perception of service to self = service to others
- Look in all areas of life

Today's Flip It:
- Balance perceived negative action/inaction until benefits = drawbacks
- Balance perceived positive action/inaction until drawbacks = benefits

My highest priority actions for tomorrow:

Observe groups who are operating in a highly productive manner and notice how they are supporting and challenging each other to achieve what they want. You will become more aware of what creates conflict in future situations. — Optimum Thinking

AUG 14

Daily Gratitude and Intention

Today I am grateful for:
- Balance perception of service to self = service to others
- Look in all areas of life

Today's Flip It:
- Balance perceived negative action/inaction until benefits = drawbacks
- Balance perceived positive action/inaction until drawbacks = benefits

My highest priority actions for tomorrow:

AUG 15

Some people grumble that roses have thorns; I am grateful that thorns have roses. — Alphonse Karr

Daily Gratitude and Intention

Today I am grateful for:
- Balance perception of service to self = service to others
- Look in all areas of life

Today's Flip It:
- Balance perceived negative action/inaction until benefits = drawbacks
- Balance perceived positive action/inaction until drawbacks = benefits

My highest priority actions for tomorrow:

Be grateful for your negative thinking; it is designed to help you work out what you DON'T want.
— Optimum Thinking

AUG 16

Daily Gratitude and Intention

Today I am grateful for:
- Balance perception of service to self = service to others
- Look in all areas of life

Today's Flip It:
- Balance perceived negative action/inaction until benefits = drawbacks
- Balance perceived positive action/inaction until drawbacks = benefits

My highest priority actions for tomorrow:

AUG 17

'Thank you' is a wonderful phrase. Use it. It will add stature to your soul. — Marjorie Pay Hinckley

Daily Gratitude and Intention

Today I am grateful for:
- Balance perception of service to self = service to others
- Look in all areas of life

Today's Flip It:
- Balance perceived negative action/inaction until benefits = drawbacks
- Balance perceived positive action/inaction until drawbacks = benefits

My highest priority actions for tomorrow:

If, at the end of a day you are feeling really proud enjoy it for a moment and then ask yourself who you could have served better today to bring yourself back to being equal to others (Optimum Dog) before you attract external humbling circumstances to do it for you. — **Optimum Thinking**

AUG 18

Daily Gratitude and Intention

Today I am grateful for:
- Balance perception of service to self = service to others
- Look in all areas of life

Today's Flip It:
- Balance perceived negative action/inaction until benefits = drawbacks
- Balance perceived positive action/inaction until drawbacks = benefits

My highest priority actions for tomorrow:

AUG 19

Thanksgiving creates abundance. — Ann Voskamp

Daily Gratitude and Intention

Today I am grateful for:
- Balance perception of service to self = service to others
- Look in all areas of life

Today's Flip It:
- Balance perceived negative action/inaction until benefits = drawbacks
- Balance perceived positive action/inaction until drawbacks = benefits

My highest priority actions for tomorrow:

When you feel a strong negative emotional charge, first ask yourself what unrealistic expectations you may have in that moment. — Optimum Thinking

AUG 20

Daily Gratitude and Intention

Today I am grateful for:
- Balance perception of service to self = service to others
- Look in all areas of life

Today's Flip It:
- Balance perceived negative action/inaction until benefits = drawbacks
- Balance perceived positive action/inaction until drawbacks = benefits

My highest priority actions for tomorrow:

AUG 21

As many people as there are to hold you back, there are angels whose humanity makes up for all the others. I've had my share of angels. — Abraham Verghese

Daily Gratitude and Intention

Today I am grateful for:
- Balance perception of service to self = service to others
- Look in all areas of life

Today's Flip It:
- Balance perceived negative action/inaction until benefits = drawbacks
- Balance perceived positive action/inaction until drawbacks = benefits

My highest priority actions for tomorrow:

If you want to create and sustain connected meaningful relationships, make sure you understand each other's goals so you can support their achievement and they can support yours. — Optimum Thinking

AUG 22

Daily Gratitude and Intention

Today I am grateful for:
- Balance perception of service to self = service to others
- Look in all areas of life

Today's Flip It:
- Balance perceived negative action/inaction until benefits = drawbacks
- Balance perceived positive action/inaction until drawbacks = benefits

My highest priority actions for tomorrow:

AUG 23

The best and most beautiful things in this world cannot be seen or even heard, but must be felt with the heart.
— Helen Keller

Daily Gratitude and Intention

Today I am grateful for:
- Balance perception of service to self = service to others
- Look in all areas of life

Today's Flip It:
- Balance perceived negative action/inaction until benefits = drawbacks
- Balance perceived positive action/inaction until drawbacks = benefits

My highest priority actions for tomorrow:

Be grateful for the people and friends who have left your life and made space for the new people who have come in to support and challenge you to keep growing.
— Optimum Thinking

AUG 24

Daily Gratitude and Intention

Today I am grateful for:
- Balance perception of service to self = service to others
- Look in all areas of life

Today's Flip It:
- Balance perceived negative action/inaction until benefits = drawbacks
- Balance perceived positive action/inaction until drawbacks = benefits

My highest priority actions for tomorrow:

AUG 25

The essence of all beautiful art, all great art, is gratitude. — Friedrich Nietzsche

Daily Gratitude and Intention

Today I am grateful for:
- Balance perception of service to self = service to others
- Look in all areas of life

Today's Flip It:
- Balance perceived negative action/inaction until benefits = drawbacks
- Balance perceived positive action/inaction until drawbacks = benefits

My highest priority actions for tomorrow:

Nothing is ever gained or lost; it changes form. If you perceive you have lost someone or some thing, find the new forms you now have it in to see that you continue to have what you want in your life.
— *Optimum Thinking*

AUG 26

Daily Gratitude and Intention

Today I am grateful for:
- Balance perception of service to self = service to others
- Look in all areas of life

Today's Flip It:
- Balance perceived negative action/inaction until benefits = drawbacks
- Balance perceived positive action/inaction until drawbacks = benefits

My highest priority actions for tomorrow:

AUG 27

The greatest wisdom is in simplicity. Love, respect, tolerance, sharing, gratitude, forgiveness. It's not complex or elaborate. The real knowledge is free. It's encoded in your DNA. All you need is within you. Great teachers have said that from the beginning. Find your heart, and you will find your way. — Carlos Barrios

Daily Gratitude and Intention

Today I am grateful for:
- Balance perception of service to self = service to others
- Look in all areas of life

Today's Flip It:
- Balance perceived negative action/inaction until benefits = drawbacks
- Balance perceived positive action/inaction until drawbacks = benefits

My highest priority actions for tomorrow:

If you fight too hard to have something it will elude you until you appreciate what you have. If you fight too hard to avoid something, you will attract it until you learn to appreciate it. — Optimum Thinking

AUG 28

Daily Gratitude and Intention

Today I am grateful for:
- Balance perception of service to self = service to others
- Look in all areas of life

Today's Flip It:
- Balance perceived negative action/inaction until benefits = drawbacks
- Balance perceived positive action/inaction until drawbacks = benefits

My highest priority actions for tomorrow:

AUG 29

The highest tribute to the dead is not grief but gratitude. — Thornton Wilder

Daily Gratitude and Intention

Today I am grateful for:
- Balance perception of service to self = service to others
- Look in all areas of life

Today's Flip It:
- Balance perceived negative action/inaction until benefits = drawbacks
- Balance perceived positive action/inaction until drawbacks = benefits

My highest priority actions for tomorrow:

> Goals need to connect with your heart, push your current capacity and be big enough to scare you a little. Then you need to make your plan clear and detailed enough to inspire you into focussed action.
> — Optimum Thinking

AUG 30

Daily Gratitude and Intention

Today I am grateful for:
- Balance perception of service to self = service to others
- Look in all areas of life

Today's Flip It:
- Balance perceived negative action/inaction until benefits = drawbacks
- Balance perceived positive action/inaction until drawbacks = benefits

My highest priority actions for tomorrow:

AUG 31

The moment one gives close attention to anything, even a blade of grass, it becomes a mysterious, awesome, indescribably magnificent world in itself.
— Henry Miller

Daily Gratitude and Intention

Today I am grateful for:
- Balance perception of service to self = service to others
- Look in all areas of life

Today's Flip It:
- Balance perceived negative action/inaction until benefits = drawbacks
- Balance perceived positive action/inaction until drawbacks = benefits

My highest priority actions for tomorrow:

SEPTEMBER

Monthly Intention Plan

Write the top priorities you intend to focus on in each area of your life during this month.

SPIRITUAL / MISSION / SELF-ACTUALIZATION

MENTAL / EDUCATION

VOCATION / CAREER

FINANCIAL WEALTH / SAVING & INVESTING

FAMILY / RELATIONSHIP

SOCIAL / FRIENDS

HEALTH & PHYSICAL APPEARANCE

SEP 1

> We learned about gratitude and humility — that so many people had a hand in our success, from the teachers who inspired us to the janitors who kept our school clean... and we were taught to value everyone's contribution and treat everyone with respect.
> — Michelle Obama

Daily Gratitude and Intention

Today I am grateful for:
- Balance perception of service to self = service to others
- Look in all areas of life

Today's Flip It:
- Balance perceived negative action/inaction until benefits = drawbacks
- Balance perceived positive action/inaction until drawbacks = benefits

My highest priority actions for tomorrow:

Negative emotions hurt you! Every time you hate someone, as you release harmful stress chemicals from your brain to your body, you truly hate yourself! — Optimum Thinking

SEP 2

Daily Gratitude and Intention

Today I am grateful for:
- Balance perception of service to self = service to others
- Look in all areas of life

Today's Flip It:
- Balance perceived negative action/inaction until benefits = drawbacks
- Balance perceived positive action/inaction until drawbacks = benefits

My highest priority actions for tomorrow:

SEP 3

Holding onto anger is like drinking poison and expecting the other person to die. — Buddha

Daily Gratitude and Intention

Today I am grateful for:
- Balance perception of service to self = service to others
- Look in all areas of life

Today's Flip It:
- Balance perceived negative action/inaction until benefits = drawbacks
- Balance perceived positive action/inaction until drawbacks = benefits

My highest priority actions for tomorrow:

> When conflict occurs, get curious about what each person's agenda really is and you will understand their behaviour more easily. Think about what each person has as their Hierarchy of Individual Life Priorities (HILP) and what is being challenged in that moment.
> — Optimum Thinking

SEP 4

Daily Gratitude and Intention

Today I am grateful for:
- Balance perception of service to self = service to others
- Look in all areas of life

Today's Flip It:
- Balance perceived negative action/inaction until benefits = drawbacks
- Balance perceived positive action/inaction until drawbacks = benefits

My highest priority actions for tomorrow:

SEP 5

The more you recognize and express gratitude for the things you have, the more things you will have to express gratitude for.
— Zig Ziglar

Daily Gratitude and Intention

Today I am grateful for:
- Balance perception of service to self = service to others
- Look in all areas of life

Today's Flip It:
- Balance perceived negative action/inaction until benefits = drawbacks
- Balance perceived positive action/inaction until drawbacks = benefits

My highest priority actions for tomorrow:

Optimum Thinking harnesses the power of positive and negative thinking to see how an event is perfect for us at that time to help us grow and learn.
— *Optimum Thinking*

SEP 6

Daily Gratitude and Intention

Today I am grateful for:
- Balance perception of service to self = service to others
- Look in all areas of life

Today's Flip It:
- Balance perceived negative action/inaction until benefits = drawbacks
- Balance perceived positive action/inaction until drawbacks = benefits

My highest priority actions for tomorrow:

SEP 7

The only people with whom you should try to get even are those who have helped you. — John E. Southard

Daily Gratitude and Intention

Today I am grateful for:
- Balance perception of service to self = service to others
- Look in all areas of life

Today's Flip It:
- Balance perceived negative action/inaction until benefits = drawbacks
- Balance perceived positive action/inaction until drawbacks = benefits

My highest priority actions for tomorrow:

Your level of frustration for not achieving is in direct proportion to your lack of planning.
— Optimum Thinking

SEP 8

Daily Gratitude and Intention

Today I am grateful for:
- Balance perception of service to self = service to others
- Look in all areas of life

Today's Flip It:
- Balance perceived negative action/inaction until benefits = drawbacks
- Balance perceived positive action/inaction until drawbacks = benefits

My highest priority actions for tomorrow:

SEP 9

The things that most deserve our gratitude we just take for granted. Without air we cannot live for more than a minute or two. Everyday we are breathing in and breathing out, but do we ever feel grateful to the air? — Sri Chinmoy

Daily Gratitude and Intention

Today I am grateful for:
- Balance perception of service to self = service to others
- Look in all areas of life

Today's Flip It:
- Balance perceived negative action/inaction until benefits = drawbacks
- Balance perceived positive action/inaction until drawbacks = benefits

My highest priority actions for tomorrow:

When you are expressing unhappiness, you are ignoring all that you have to be grateful for. — Optimum Thinking

SEP 10

Daily Gratitude and Intention

Today I am grateful for:
- Balance perception of service to self = service to others
- Look in all areas of life

Today's Flip It:
- Balance perceived negative action/inaction until benefits = drawbacks
- Balance perceived positive action/inaction until drawbacks = benefits

My highest priority actions for tomorrow:

SEP 11

Gratitude is looking on the brighter side of life, even if it means hurting your eyes. — Ellen DeGeneres

Daily Gratitude and Intention

Today I am grateful for:
- Balance perception of service to self = service to others
- Look in all areas of life

Today's Flip It:
- Balance perceived negative action/inaction until benefits = drawbacks
- Balance perceived positive action/inaction until drawbacks = benefits

My highest priority actions for tomorrow:

People stay in quality relationships when they are both truly grateful for how they support and challenge each other to connect, grow and achieve their highest individual life priorities. — Optimum Thinking

SEP 12

Daily Gratitude and Intention

Today I am grateful for:
- Balance perception of service to self = service to others
- Look in all areas of life

Today's Flip It:
- Balance perceived negative action/inaction until benefits = drawbacks
- Balance perceived positive action/inaction until drawbacks = benefits

My highest priority actions for tomorrow:

SEP 13

There are only two ways to live your life. One is as though nothing is a miracle. The other is as though everything is a miracle. — Albert Einstein

Daily Gratitude and Intention

Today I am grateful for:
- Balance perception of service to self = service to others
- Look in all areas of life

Today's Flip It:
- Balance perceived negative action/inaction until benefits = drawbacks
- Balance perceived positive action/inaction until drawbacks = benefits

My highest priority actions for tomorrow:

Fail to Plan = Plan to Fail

SEP 14

Daily Gratitude and Intention

Today I am grateful for:
- Balance perception of service to self = service to others
- Look in all areas of life

Today's Flip It:
- Balance perceived negative action/inaction until benefits = drawbacks
- Balance perceived positive action/inaction until drawbacks = benefits

My highest priority actions for tomorrow:

SEP 15

There is a law of gratitude, and it is... the natural principle that action and reaction are always equal and in opposite directions. The grateful outreaching of your mind in thankful praise to supreme intelligence is a liberation or expenditure of force. It cannot fail to reach that to which it is addressed, and the reaction is an instantaneous movement toward you. — **Wally Wattles**

Daily Gratitude and Intention

Today I am grateful for:
- Balance perception of service to self = service to others
- Look in all areas of life

Today's Flip It:
- Balance perceived negative action/inaction until benefits = drawbacks
- Balance perceived positive action/inaction until drawbacks = benefits

My highest priority actions for tomorrow:

There is always the exact opposite positive in any perceived negative behaviour occuring at the exact same moment. Practice finding it in little moments and it will help you balance the bigger challenges faster.
— Optimum Thinking

SEP 16

Daily Gratitude and Intention

Today I am grateful for:
- Balance perception of service to self = service to others
- Look in all areas of life

Today's Flip It:
- Balance perceived negative action/inaction until benefits = drawbacks
- Balance perceived positive action/inaction until drawbacks = benefits

My highest priority actions for tomorrow:

SEP 17

There is as much greatness of mind in acknowledging a good turn, as in doing it.
— Seneca

Daily Gratitude and Intention

Today I am grateful for:
- Balance perception of service to self = service to others
- Look in all areas of life

Today's Flip It:
- Balance perceived negative action/inaction until benefits = drawbacks
- Balance perceived positive action/inaction until drawbacks = benefits

My highest priority actions for tomorrow:

No one can make you feel anything. Owning and understanding this is fundamental to mastering your emotions. — Optimum Thinking

SEP 18

Daily Gratitude and Intention

Today I am grateful for:
- Balance perception of service to self = service to others
- Look in all areas of life

Today's Flip It:
- Balance perceived negative action/inaction until benefits = drawbacks
- Balance perceived positive action/inaction until drawbacks = benefits

My highest priority actions for tomorrow:

SEP 19

There is nothing better than the encouragement of a good friend. — Jean Jacques Rousseau

Daily Gratitude and Intention

Today I am grateful for:
- Balance perception of service to self = service to others
- Look in all areas of life

Today's Flip It:
- Balance perceived negative action/inaction until benefits = drawbacks
- Balance perceived positive action/inaction until drawbacks = benefits

My highest priority actions for tomorrow:

We are all Meaning Making Machines. We create our emotions with the meanings we make about what we perceive to have happened. — Optimum Thinking

SEP 20

Daily Gratitude and Intention

Today I am grateful for:
- Balance perception of service to self = service to others
- Look in all areas of life

Today's Flip It:
- Balance perceived negative action/inaction until benefits = drawbacks
- Balance perceived positive action/inaction until drawbacks = benefits

My highest priority actions for tomorrow:

SEP 21

There is only one thing that can form a bond between men, and that is gratitude...we cannot give someone else greater power over us than we have ourselves.
— Charles de Secondat

Daily Gratitude and Intention

Today I am grateful for:
- Balance perception of service to self = service to others
- Look in all areas of life

Today's Flip It:
- Balance perceived negative action/inaction until benefits = drawbacks
- Balance perceived positive action/inaction until drawbacks = benefits

My highest priority actions for tomorrow:

Every action or inaction we choose is a strategy to get what we want. — Optimum Thinking

SEP 22

Daily Gratitude and Intention

Today I am grateful for:
- Balance perception of service to self = service to others
- Look in all areas of life

Today's Flip It:
- Balance perceived negative action/inaction until benefits = drawbacks
- Balance perceived positive action/inaction until drawbacks = benefits

My highest priority actions for tomorrow:

SEP 23

They do not love, that do not show their love.
— William Shakespeare

Daily Gratitude and Intention

Today I am grateful for:
- Balance perception of service to self = service to others
- Look in all areas of life

Today's Flip It:
- Balance perceived negative action/inaction until benefits = drawbacks
- Balance perceived positive action/inaction until drawbacks = benefits

My highest priority actions for tomorrow:

The only "perfect" you are meant to be is "perfectly you"! That is something only you can achieve.
— Optimum Thinking

SEP 24

Daily Gratitude and Intention

Today I am grateful for:
- Balance perception of service to self = service to others
- Look in all areas of life

Today's Flip It:
- Balance perceived negative action/inaction until benefits = drawbacks
- Balance perceived positive action/inaction until drawbacks = benefits

My highest priority actions for tomorrow:

SEP 25

Though they only take a second to say, thank you's leave a warm feeling behind that can last for hours.
— Kent Allan Rees

Daily Gratitude and Intention

Today I am grateful for:
- Balance perception of service to self = service to others
- Look in all areas of life

Today's Flip It:
- Balance perceived negative action/inaction until benefits = drawbacks
- Balance perceived positive action/inaction until drawbacks = benefits

My highest priority actions for tomorrow:

There is no such thing as "good" people and "bad" people. It is more empowering to see everyone as an "Agent of the Universe" with a hierarchy of individual life priorities (HILP) trying to get what they want. — **Optimum Thinking**

SEP 26

Daily Gratitude and Intention

Today I am grateful for:
- Balance perception of service to self = service to others
- Look in all areas of life

Today's Flip It:
- Balance perceived negative action/inaction until benefits = drawbacks
- Balance perceived positive action/inaction until drawbacks = benefits

My highest priority actions for tomorrow:

SEP 27

> To educate yourself for the feeling of gratitude means to take nothing for granted, but to always seek out and value the kind that will stand behind the action. Nothing that is done for you is a matter of course. Everything originates in a will for the good, which is directed at you. Train yourself never to put off the word or action for the expression of gratitude. — Albert Schweitzer

Daily Gratitude and Intention

Today I am grateful for:
- Balance perception of service to self = service to others
- Look in all areas of life

Today's Flip It:
- Balance perceived negative action/inaction until benefits = drawbacks
- Balance perceived positive action/inaction until drawbacks = benefits

My highest priority actions for tomorrow:

We all possess every action and inaction we list on our polarized "good person" and "bad person" list and we choose to use whatever we believe will get us the best result in the moment. — Optimum Thinking

SEP 28

Daily Gratitude and Intention

Today I am grateful for:
- Balance perception of service to self = service to others
- Look in all areas of life

Today's Flip It:
- Balance perceived negative action/inaction until benefits = drawbacks
- Balance perceived positive action/inaction until drawbacks = benefits

My highest priority actions for tomorrow:

SEP 29

> Do the difficult things while they are easy and do the great things while they are small. A journey of a thousand miles must begin with a single step.
> — Lao Tzu

Daily Gratitude and Intention

Today I am grateful for:
- Balance perception of service to self = service to others
- Look in all areas of life

Today's Flip It:
- Balance perceived negative action/inaction until benefits = drawbacks
- Balance perceived positive action/inaction until drawbacks = benefits

My highest priority actions for tomorrow:

Overdogs attract humbling circumstances. If you feel yourself puffing up and getting proud, ask yourself the right questions to bring you back to balance before external forces do. — Optimum Thinking

SEP 30

Daily Gratitude and Intention

Today I am grateful for:
- Balance perception of service to self = service to others
- Look in all areas of life

Today's Flip It:
- Balance perceived negative action/inaction until benefits = drawbacks
- Balance perceived positive action/inaction until drawbacks = benefits

My highest priority actions for tomorrow:

OCTOBER

Monthly Intention Plan

Write the top priorities you intend to focus on in each area of your life during this month.

SPIRITUAL / MISSION / SELF-ACTUALIZATION

MENTAL / EDUCATION

VOCATION / CAREER

FINANCIAL WEALTH / SAVING & INVESTING

FAMILY / RELATIONSHIP

SOCIAL / FRIENDS

HEALTH & PHYSICAL APPEARANCE

OCT 1

Happiness is not a goal, it is a by-product. Paradoxically, the one sure way not to be happy is deliberately to map out a way of life in which one would please oneself completely and exclusively. — Eleanor Roosevelt

Daily Gratitude and Intention

Today I am grateful for:
- Balance perception of service to self = service to others
- Look in all areas of life

Today's Flip It:
- Balance perceived negative action/inaction until benefits = drawbacks
- Balance perceived positive action/inaction until drawbacks = benefits

My highest priority actions for tomorrow:

We each use whatever action or inaction we believe will give us the most benefit at the time...so does everyone else.
— Optimum Thinking

OCT 2

Daily Gratitude and Intention

Today I am grateful for:
- Balance perception of service to self = service to others
- Look in all areas of life

Today's Flip It:
- Balance perceived negative action/inaction until benefits = drawbacks
- Balance perceived positive action/inaction until drawbacks = benefits

My highest priority actions for tomorrow:

OCT 3

Wake at dawn with a winged heart and give thanks for another day of loving.
— Kahlil Gibran

Daily Gratitude and Intention

Today I am grateful for:
- Balance perception of service to self = service to others
- Look in all areas of life

Today's Flip It:
- Balance perceived negative action/inaction until benefits = drawbacks
- Balance perceived positive action/inaction until drawbacks = benefits

My highest priority actions for tomorrow:

Gratitude includes being able to give thanks for the lessons and benefits in the challenges to the point you appreciate that there is nothing to forgive. — Optimum Thinking

OCT 4

Daily Gratitude and Intention

Today I am grateful for:
- Balance perception of service to self = service to others
- Look in all areas of life

Today's Flip It:
- Balance perceived negative action/inaction until benefits = drawbacks
- Balance perceived positive action/inaction until drawbacks = benefits

My highest priority actions for tomorrow:

OCT 5

Cherish forever what makes you unique, 'cuz you're really a yawn if it goes. — Bette Midler

Daily Gratitude and Intention

Today I am grateful for:
- Balance perception of service to self = service to others
- Look in all areas of life

Today's Flip It:
- Balance perceived negative action/inaction until benefits = drawbacks
- Balance perceived positive action/inaction until drawbacks = benefits

My highest priority actions for tomorrow:

Practice your Optimum Thinking daily and harness the power of positive and negative thinking. — Optimum Thinking

OCT 6

Daily Gratitude and Intention

Today I am grateful for:
- Balance perception of service to self = service to others
- Look in all areas of life

Today's Flip It:
- Balance perceived negative action/inaction until benefits = drawbacks
- Balance perceived positive action/inaction until drawbacks = benefits

My highest priority actions for tomorrow:

OCT 7

Rock bottom became the solid foundation on which I rebuilt my life. — J. K. Rowlings

Daily Gratitude and Intention

Today I am grateful for:
- Balance perception of service to self = service to others
- Look in all areas of life

Today's Flip It:
- Balance perceived negative action/inaction until benefits = drawbacks
- Balance perceived positive action/inaction until drawbacks = benefits

My highest priority actions for tomorrow:

Optimum Dogs are humbly empowered, know what they want and are prepared to embrace both support and challenge to achieve their mission. — Optimum Thinking

OCT 8

Daily Gratitude and Intention

Today I am grateful for:
- Balance perception of service to self = service to others
- Look in all areas of life

Today's Flip It:
- Balance perceived negative action/inaction until benefits = drawbacks
- Balance perceived positive action/inaction until drawbacks = benefits

My highest priority actions for tomorrow:

OCT 9

We must find time to stop and thank the people who make a difference in our lives.
— John F. Kennedy

Daily Gratitude and Intention

Today I am grateful for:
- Balance perception of service to self = service to others
- Look in all areas of life

Today's Flip It:
- Balance perceived negative action/inaction until benefits = drawbacks
- Balance perceived positive action/inaction until drawbacks = benefits

My highest priority actions for tomorrow:

Competitors compete with each other. Champions compete with themselves. — Optimum Thinking

OCT 10

Daily Gratitude and Intention

Today I am grateful for:
- Balance perception of service to self = service to others
- Look in all areas of life

Today's Flip It:
- Balance perceived negative action/inaction until benefits = drawbacks
- Balance perceived positive action/inaction until drawbacks = benefits

My highest priority actions for tomorrow:

OCT 11

We should certainly count our blessings, but we should also make our blessings count. — Neal A. Maxwell

Daily Gratitude and Intention

Today I am grateful for:
- Balance perception of service to self = service to others
- Look in all areas of life

Today's Flip It:
- Balance perceived negative action/inaction until benefits = drawbacks
- Balance perceived positive action/inaction until drawbacks = benefits

My highest priority actions for tomorrow:

If you are doing a 'pity party' take the time to list what you are grateful for in all areas of your life. Keep this list, re-read it and add to it any time in the future you find yourself slipping into a negative state. There is always fair exchange. — Optimum Thinking

OCT 12

Daily Gratitude and Intention

Today I am grateful for:
- Balance perception of service to self = service to others
- Look in all areas of life

Today's Flip It:
- Balance perceived negative action/inaction until benefits = drawbacks
- Balance perceived positive action/inaction until drawbacks = benefits

My highest priority actions for tomorrow:

OCT 13

What I've learned is there's a scientifically proven phenomenon that's attached to gratitude, and that if you consciously take note of what is good in your life, quantifiable benefits happen. — Deborah Norville

Daily Gratitude and Intention

Today I am grateful for:
- Balance perception of service to self = service to others
- Look in all areas of life

Today's Flip It:
- Balance perceived negative action/inaction until benefits = drawbacks
- Balance perceived positive action/inaction until drawbacks = benefits

My highest priority actions for tomorrow:

Infatuation keeps us stuck in fantasy and reduces our ability to live in and appreciate the present and the gifts life has already given us. — Optimum Thinking

OCT 14

Daily Gratitude and Intention

Today I am grateful for:
- Balance perception of service to self = service to others
- Look in all areas of life

Today's Flip It:
- Balance perceived negative action/inaction until benefits = drawbacks
- Balance perceived positive action/inaction until drawbacks = benefits

My highest priority actions for tomorrow:

OCT 15

What you focus on expands, and when you focus on the goodness in your life, you create more of it. Opportunities, relationships, even money flowed my way when I learned to be grateful no matter what happened in my life. — Oprah Winfrey

Daily Gratitude and Intention

Today I am grateful for:
- Balance perception of service to self = service to others
- Look in all areas of life

Today's Flip It:
- Balance perceived negative action/inaction until benefits = drawbacks
- Balance perceived positive action/inaction until drawbacks = benefits

My highest priority actions for tomorrow:

Find the gifts and lessons in every challenge you perceive. Overcoming the challenges is what births your leadership and develops your problem-solving and resilience. — Optimum Thinking

OCT 16

Daily Gratitude and Intention

Today I am grateful for:
- Balance perception of service to self = service to others
- Look in all areas of life

Today's Flip It:
- Balance perceived negative action/inaction until benefits = drawbacks
- Balance perceived positive action/inaction until drawbacks = benefits

My highest priority actions for tomorrow:

OCT 17

Whatever our individual troubles and challenges may be, it's important to pause every now and then to appreciate all that we have, on every level. We need to literally "count our blessings," give thanks for them, allow ourselves to enjoy them, and relish the experience of prosperity we already have. — Shakti Gawain

Daily Gratitude and Intention

Today I am grateful for:
- Balance perception of service to self = service to others
- Look in all areas of life

Today's Flip It:
- Balance perceived negative action/inaction until benefits = drawbacks
- Balance perceived positive action/inaction until drawbacks = benefits

My highest priority actions for tomorrow:

The only constant is transformation. Take the time to find equal benefits and drawbacks in any transformation you perceive in your life as they occur. This will help you stay balanced, grateful and vital. — Optimum Thinking

OCT 18

Daily Gratitude and Intention

Today I am grateful for:
- Balance perception of service to self = service to others
- Look in all areas of life

Today's Flip It:
- Balance perceived negative action/inaction until benefits = drawbacks
- Balance perceived positive action/inaction until drawbacks = benefits

My highest priority actions for tomorrow:

OCT 19

When it comes to life the critical thing is whether you take things for granted or take them with gratitude.
— Gilbert K. Chesterton

Daily Gratitude and Intention

Today I am grateful for:
- Balance perception of service to self = service to others
- Look in all areas of life

Today's Flip It:
- Balance perceived negative action/inaction until benefits = drawbacks
- Balance perceived positive action/inaction until drawbacks = benefits

My highest priority actions for tomorrow:

Separate perceived negative actions/inactions from the person. The action is no more than a tool the person is using to try to get what they want. Choose to perceive the balance in the action and still love the person.
— Optimum Thinking

OCT 20

Daily Gratitude and Intention

Today I am grateful for:
- Balance perception of service to self = service to others
- Look in all areas of life

Today's Flip It:
- Balance perceived negative action/inaction until benefits = drawbacks
- Balance perceived positive action/inaction until drawbacks = benefits

My highest priority actions for tomorrow:

OCT 21

When we become more fully aware that our success is due in large measure to the loyalty, helpfulness, and encouragement we have received from others, our desire grows to pass on similar gifts. Gratitude spurs us on to prove ourselves worthy of what others have done for us. The spirit of gratitude is a powerful energizer.
— Wilferd A. Peterson

Daily Gratitude and Intention

Today I am grateful for:
- Balance perception of service to self = service to others
- Look in all areas of life

Today's Flip It:
- Balance perceived negative action/inaction until benefits = drawbacks
- Balance perceived positive action/inaction until drawbacks = benefits

My highest priority actions for tomorrow:

How would you treat the environment when you have certainty that you will reincarnate repeatedly and never know who you will return as? — Optimum Thinking

OCT 22

Daily Gratitude and Intention

Today I am grateful for:
- Balance perception of service to self = service to others
- Look in all areas of life

Today's Flip It:
- Balance perceived negative action/inaction until benefits = drawbacks
- Balance perceived positive action/inaction until drawbacks = benefits

My highest priority actions for tomorrow:

OCT 23

Cherish your vision and your dreams as they are the children of your soul; the blueprints of your ultimate achievements. — Napoleon Hill

Daily Gratitude and Intention

Today I am grateful for:
- Balance perception of service to self = service to others
- Look in all areas of life

Today's Flip It:
- Balance perceived negative action/inaction until benefits = drawbacks
- Balance perceived positive action/inaction until drawbacks = benefits

My highest priority actions for tomorrow:

How would you treat other people and races when you have certainty that you will reincarnate repeatedly and never know who you will return as? — Optimum Thinking

OCT 24

Daily Gratitude and Intention

Today I am grateful for:
- Balance perception of service to self = service to others
- Look in all areas of life

Today's Flip It:
- Balance perceived negative action/inaction until benefits = drawbacks
- Balance perceived positive action/inaction until drawbacks = benefits

My highest priority actions for tomorrow:

OCT 25

When we were children we were grateful to those who filled our stockings at Christmas time. Why are we not grateful to God for filling our stockings with legs?
— G.K. Chesterton

Daily Gratitude and Intention

Today I am grateful for:
- Balance perception of service to self = service to others
- Look in all areas of life

Today's Flip It:
- Balance perceived negative action/inaction until benefits = drawbacks
- Balance perceived positive action/inaction until drawbacks = benefits

My highest priority actions for tomorrow:

We are all Double Agents of the Universe both supporting and challenging each other to transform and achieve our Optimum Life Missions. — Optimum Thinking

OCT 26

Daily Gratitude and Intention

Today I am grateful for:
- Balance perception of service to self = service to others
- Look in all areas of life

Today's Flip It:
- Balance perceived negative action/inaction until benefits = drawbacks
- Balance perceived positive action/inaction until drawbacks = benefits

My highest priority actions for tomorrow:

OCT 27

When you are grateful fear disappears and abundance appears. — Tony Robbins

Daily Gratitude and Intention

Today I am grateful for:
- Balance perception of service to self = service to others
- Look in all areas of life

Today's Flip It:
- Balance perceived negative action/inaction until benefits = drawbacks
- Balance perceived positive action/inaction until drawbacks = benefits

My highest priority actions for tomorrow:

Entitlement and unrealistic expectations decay our relationships, society and economy. A service-to-self that is equal to service-to-others and expression of gratitude transforms us all to a higher level. — **Optimum Thinking**

OCT 28

Daily Gratitude and Intention

Today I am grateful for:
- Balance perception of service to self = service to others
- Look in all areas of life

Today's Flip It:
- Balance perceived negative action/inaction until benefits = drawbacks
- Balance perceived positive action/inaction until drawbacks = benefits

My highest priority actions for tomorrow:

OCT 29

Learn to remember you've got great friends, don't forget that and they will always care for you no matter what. Always remember to smile and look up at what you got in life. — Marilyn Monroe

Daily Gratitude and Intention

Today I am grateful for:
- Balance perception of service to self = service to others
- Look in all areas of life

Today's Flip It:
- Balance perceived negative action/inaction until benefits = drawbacks
- Balance perceived positive action/inaction until drawbacks = benefits

My highest priority actions for tomorrow:

Completing your annual and monthly planning is a powerful way to assess what is really important to you. You will have real evidence of where you actually have choosen to invest your resources and help you clarify what you want moving forward. — Optimum Thinking

OCT 30

Daily Gratitude and Intention

Today I am grateful for:
- Balance perception of service to self = service to others
- Look in all areas of life

Today's Flip It:
- Balance perceived negative action/inaction until benefits = drawbacks
- Balance perceived positive action/inaction until drawbacks = benefits

My highest priority actions for tomorrow:

OCT 31

Each morning, let your gratitude rise with with the sun. — Optimum Thinking

Daily Gratitude and Intention

Today I am grateful for:
- Balance perception of service to self = service to others
- Look in all areas of life

Today's Flip It:
- Balance perceived negative action/inaction until benefits = drawbacks
- Balance perceived positive action/inaction until drawbacks = benefits

My highest priority actions for tomorrow:

NOVEMBER

Monthly Intention Plan

Write the top priorities you intend to focus on in each area of your life during this month.

SPIRITUAL / MISSION / SELF-ACTUALIZATION

MENTAL / EDUCATION

VOCATION / CAREER

FINANCIAL WEALTH / SAVING & INVESTING

FAMILY / RELATIONSHIP

SOCIAL / FRIENDS

HEALTH & PHYSICAL APPEARANCE

NOV 1

*Wherever I have knocked, a door has opened.
Wherever I have wandered, a path has appeared.*
— Alice Walker

Daily Gratitude and Intention

Today I am grateful for:
- Balance perception of service to self = service to others
- Look in all areas of life

Today's Flip It:
- Balance perceived negative action/inaction until benefits = drawbacks
- Balance perceived positive action/inaction until drawbacks = benefits

My highest priority actions for tomorrow:

You program yourself with the words you use. Watch out for "victim language". When you blame others for what you have attracted into your life you are giving your power away. If you have attracted challenges there are benefits in it for you, if you take the time to think hard and find them.
— Optimum Thinking

NOV 2

Daily Gratitude and Intention

Today I am grateful for:
- Balance perception of service to self = service to others
- Look in all areas of life

Today's Flip It:
- Balance perceived negative action/inaction until benefits = drawbacks
- Balance perceived positive action/inaction until drawbacks = benefits

My highest priority actions for tomorrow:

NOV 3

Who does not thank for little will not thank for much.
— Estonian Proverb

Daily Gratitude and Intention

Today I am grateful for:
- Balance perception of service to self = service to others
- Look in all areas of life

Today's Flip It:
- Balance perceived negative action/inaction until benefits = drawbacks
- Balance perceived positive action/inaction until drawbacks = benefits

My highest priority actions for tomorrow:

If you seek a life that is happy all of the time, you are setting yourself up for failure. Instead seek a fulfilled like where you embrace both challenge and support to get what you want.
— Optimum Thinking

NOV 4

Daily Gratitude and Intention

Today I am grateful for:
- Balance perception of service to self = service to others
- Look in all areas of life

Today's Flip It:
- Balance perceived negative action/inaction until benefits = drawbacks
- Balance perceived positive action/inaction until drawbacks = benefits

My highest priority actions for tomorrow:

NOV 5

You pray in your distress and in your need; would that you might pray also in the fullness of your joy and in your days of abundance. — Kahlil Gibran

Daily Gratitude and Intention

Today I am grateful for:
- Balance perception of service to self = service to others
- Look in all areas of life

Today's Flip It:
- Balance perceived negative action/inaction until benefits = drawbacks
- Balance perceived positive action/inaction until drawbacks = benefits

My highest priority actions for tomorrow:

There is only one person who can give you "self-esteem". If you are beating yourself up, find where you know you have skills and abilities that are above other people until you perceive you are equal to others and perfectly, uniquely you. — Optimum Thinking

NOV 6

Daily Gratitude and Intention

Today I am grateful for:
- Balance perception of service to self = service to others
- Look in all areas of life

Today's Flip It:
- Balance perceived negative action/inaction until benefits = drawbacks
- Balance perceived positive action/inaction until drawbacks = benefits

My highest priority actions for tomorrow:

NOV 7

You simply will not be the same person two months from now after consciously giving thanks each day for the abundance that exists in your life. And you will have set in motion an ancient spiritual law: the more you have and are grateful for, the more will be given you. — Sarah Ban Breathnach

Daily Gratitude and Intention

Today I am grateful for:
- Balance perception of service to self = service to others
- Look in all areas of life

Today's Flip It:
- Balance perceived negative action/inaction until benefits = drawbacks
- Balance perceived positive action/inaction until drawbacks = benefits

My highest priority actions for tomorrow:

> There is a divine intelligence that is beyond our comprehension that is running this show we call life. The wisdom of this intelligence has set us up to strive to achieve, learn and grow. When you are wallowing in a 'pity party' you have forgotten your purpose and what it will take to achieve it. Set goals and get your hands back on the steering wheel of your life!
> — Optimum Thinking

NOV 8

Daily Gratitude and Intention

Today I am grateful for:
- Balance perception of service to self = service to others
- Look in all areas of life

Today's Flip It:
- Balance perceived negative action/inaction until benefits = drawbacks
- Balance perceived positive action/inaction until drawbacks = benefits

My highest priority actions for tomorrow:

NOV 9

Many of us spend half our time wishing for things that we could have if we didn't spend half our time wishing.
— Alexander Woollcott

Daily Gratitude and Intention

Today I am grateful for:
- Balance perception of service to self = service to others
- Look in all areas of life

Today's Flip It:
- Balance perceived negative action/inaction until benefits = drawbacks
- Balance perceived positive action/inaction until drawbacks = benefits

My highest priority actions for tomorrow:

When a parent sets a boundary for their child, it is because they love them enough to do something the child may perceive as 'bad'. Understanding boundaries is critical for us to live as a family and society. — Optimum Thinking

NOV 10

Daily Gratitude and Intention

Today I am grateful for:
- Balance perception of service to self = service to others
- Look in all areas of life

Today's Flip It:
- Balance perceived negative action/inaction until benefits = drawbacks
- Balance perceived positive action/inaction until drawbacks = benefits

My highest priority actions for tomorrow:

NOV 11

If you do a good job for others, you heal yourself at the same time because a dose of joy is a spiritual cure. It transcends all barriers. — Ed Sullivan

Daily Gratitude and Intention

Today I am grateful for:
- Balance perception of service to self = service to others
- Look in all areas of life

Today's Flip It:
- Balance perceived negative action/inaction until benefits = drawbacks
- Balance perceived positive action/inaction until drawbacks = benefits

My highest priority actions for tomorrow:

If you are not achieving a goal, assess why you haven't. If it is too big, break it down into smaller steps. If it is not important enough to you, delete it. Live the life you consciously choose! — **Optimum Thinking**

NOV 12

Daily Gratitude and Intention

Today I am grateful for:
- Balance perception of service to self = service to others
- Look in all areas of life

Today's Flip It:
- Balance perceived negative action/inaction until benefits = drawbacks
- Balance perceived positive action/inaction until drawbacks = benefits

My highest priority actions for tomorrow:

NOV 13

You already have everything your heart desires.
— Traditional proverb

Daily Gratitude and Intention

Today I am grateful for:
- Balance perception of service to self = service to others
- Look in all areas of life

....
....
....
....
....
....
....
....
....
....
....
....

Today's Flip It:
- Balance perceived negative action/inaction until benefits = drawbacks
- Balance perceived positive action/inaction until drawbacks = benefits

....
....
....
....
....

My highest priority actions for tomorrow:
....
....
....
....
....

Expressing our gratitude helps us appreciate that we truly are already living our life purpose every day. — Optimum Thinking

NOV 14

Daily Gratitude and Intention

Today I am grateful for:
- Balance perception of service to self = service to others
- Look in all areas of life

Today's Flip It:
- Balance perceived negative action/inaction until benefits = drawbacks
- Balance perceived positive action/inaction until drawbacks = benefits

My highest priority actions for tomorrow:

NOV 15

Circumstances may be likened to stones — you can use them to build with, or you can let them weigh you down.
— John Demartini

Daily Gratitude and Intention

Today I am grateful for:
- Balance perception of service to self = service to others
- Look in all areas of life

Today's Flip It:
- Balance perceived negative action/inaction until benefits = drawbacks
- Balance perceived positive action/inaction until drawbacks = benefits

My highest priority actions for tomorrow:

You live your Optimum Life when you consciously choose what you want, plan how to get it and learn to clear emotional charge that gets in the way. — Optimum Thinking

NOV 16

Daily Gratitude and Intention

Today I am grateful for:
- Balance perception of service to self = service to others
- Look in all areas of life

Today's Flip It:
- Balance perceived negative action/inaction until benefits = drawbacks
- Balance perceived positive action/inaction until drawbacks = benefits

My highest priority actions for tomorrow:

NOV 17

To see your drama clearly is to be liberated from it. — Ken Keyes Jr

Daily Gratitude and Intention

Today I am grateful for:
- Balance perception of service to self = service to others
- Look in all areas of life

Today's Flip It:
- Balance perceived negative action/inaction until benefits = drawbacks
- Balance perceived positive action/inaction until drawbacks = benefits

My highest priority actions for tomorrow:

If you perceive something is "too good to be true" then it is time to do some work and find all of the drawbacks to it until you can see it has both sides equally. If you don't, you will be gullible and likely to be overpowered in some way.
— *Optimum Thinking*

NOV 18

Daily Gratitude and Intention

Today I am grateful for:
- Balance perception of service to self = service to others
- Look in all areas of life

Today's Flip It:
- Balance perceived negative action/inaction until benefits = drawbacks
- Balance perceived positive action/inaction until drawbacks = benefits

My highest priority actions for tomorrow:

NOV 19

If you haven't got all the things you want, be grateful for the things you don't have that you don't want.
— Anonymous

Daily Gratitude and Intention

Today I am grateful for:
- Balance perception of service to self = service to others
- Look in all areas of life

Today's Flip It:
- Balance perceived negative action/inaction until benefits = drawbacks
- Balance perceived positive action/inaction until drawbacks = benefits

My highest priority actions for tomorrow:

Life wasn't meant to be easy. It is meant to be fulfilling. You will never feel fulfilled if you haven't set yourself challenges and overcome them! — *Optimum Thinking*

NOV 20

Daily Gratitude and Intention

Today I am grateful for:
- Balance perception of service to self = service to others
- Look in all areas of life

Today's Flip It:
- Balance perceived negative action/inaction until benefits = drawbacks
- Balance perceived positive action/inaction until drawbacks = benefits

My highest priority actions for tomorrow:

NOV 21

To find yourself, think for yourself. — Socrates

Daily Gratitude and Intention

Today I am grateful for:
- Balance perception of service to self = service to others
- Look in all areas of life

Today's Flip It:
- Balance perceived negative action/inaction until benefits = drawbacks
- Balance perceived positive action/inaction until drawbacks = benefits

My highest priority actions for tomorrow:

If you perceive you had a boring day today, think about what you may have missed out on by not managing your emotional state and intention. — Optimum Thinking

NOV 22

Daily Gratitude and Intention

Today I am grateful for:
- Balance perception of service to self = service to others
- Look in all areas of life

Today's Flip It:
- Balance perceived negative action/inaction until benefits = drawbacks
- Balance perceived positive action/inaction until drawbacks = benefits

My highest priority actions for tomorrow:

NOV 23

Inspiring messages are available at every moment; just be truly grateful and listen with your heart.
— John Demartini

Daily Gratitude and Intention

Today I am grateful for:
- Balance perception of service to self = service to others
- Look in all areas of life

Today's Flip It:
- Balance perceived negative action/inaction until benefits = drawbacks
- Balance perceived positive action/inaction until drawbacks = benefits

My highest priority actions for tomorrow:

> Optimum Thinking skills take work. The more you put in, the more you accelerate your achievements and relationships. — *Optimum Thinking*.

NOV 24

Daily Gratitude and Intention

Today I am grateful for:
- Balance perception of service to self = service to others
- Look in all areas of life

Today's Flip It:
- Balance perceived negative action/inaction until benefits = drawbacks
- Balance perceived positive action/inaction until drawbacks = benefits

My highest priority actions for tomorrow:

NOV 25

No act of kindness, no matter how small, is ever wasted. — Aesop

Daily Gratitude and Intention

Today I am grateful for:
- Balance perception of service to self = service to others
- Look in all areas of life

Today's Flip It:
- Balance perceived negative action/inaction until benefits = drawbacks
- Balance perceived positive action/inaction until drawbacks = benefits

My highest priority actions for tomorrow:

Plan your Optimum Life and live your love. Don't blame other people for not getting what you want. They are all busy working on getting what they want! — *Optimum Thinking*

NOV 26

Daily Gratitude and Intention

Today I am grateful for:
- Balance perception of service to self = service to others
- Look in all areas of life

Today's Flip It:
- Balance perceived negative action/inaction until benefits = drawbacks
- Balance perceived positive action/inaction until drawbacks = benefits

My highest priority actions for tomorrow:

NOV 27

It is not love, but lack of love, which is blind.
— Glenway Westcott

Daily Gratitude and Intention

Today I am grateful for:
- Balance perception of service to self = service to others
- Look in all areas of life

Today's Flip It:
- Balance perceived negative action/inaction until benefits = drawbacks
- Balance perceived positive action/inaction until drawbacks = benefits

My highest priority actions for tomorrow:

Our language is full of polarization that encourages emotional reactions. Try using hyphens to find more balanced language e.g. humbly-empowered. — Optimum Thinking

NOV 28

Daily Gratitude and Intention

Today I am grateful for:
- Balance perception of service to self = service to others
- Look in all areas of life

Today's Flip It:
- Balance perceived negative action/inaction until benefits = drawbacks
- Balance perceived positive action/inaction until drawbacks = benefits

My highest priority actions for tomorrow:

NOV 29

The people we are in relationship with are always a mirror, reflecting our own beliefs and simultaneously we are mirrors reflecting their beliefs. So relationship is one of the most powerful tools for growth...If we look honestly at our relationships we can see so much about how we created them. — Shakti Gawain

Daily Gratitude and Intention

Today I am grateful for:
- Balance perception of service to self = service to others
- Look in all areas of life

Today's Flip It:
- Balance perceived negative action/inaction until benefits = drawbacks
- Balance perceived positive action/inaction until drawbacks = benefits

My highest priority actions for tomorrow:

Gratitude, joy, inspiration and enthusiasm are the emotional states of an open heart. — Optimum Thinking

NOV 30

Daily Gratitude and Intention

Today I am grateful for:
- Balance perception of service to self = service to others
- Look in all areas of life

Today's Flip It:
- Balance perceived negative action/inaction until benefits = drawbacks
- Balance perceived positive action/inaction until drawbacks = benefits

My highest priority actions for tomorrow:

DECEMBER

Monthly Intention Plan

Write the top priorities you intend to focus on in each area of your life during this month.

SPIRITUAL / MISSION / SELF-ACTUALIZATION

MENTAL / EDUCATION

VOCATION / CAREER

FINANCIAL WEALTH / SAVING & INVESTING

FAMILY / RELATIONSHIP

SOCIAL / FRIENDS

HEALTH & PHYSICAL APPEARANCE

DEC 1

Self-reflection is the school of wisdom.
— Baltasar Gracian y Morales

Daily Gratitude and Intention

Today I am grateful for:
- Balance perception of service to self = service to others
- Look in all areas of life

Today's Flip It:
- Balance perceived negative action/inaction until benefits = drawbacks
- Balance perceived positive action/inaction until drawbacks = benefits

My highest priority actions for tomorrow:

Overdogs have care-less relationships. Underdogs are too care-ful in relationships and feel like they are treading on egg shells. Optimum dogs have caring relationships. They see their partner as equal and both challenge and support them to grow and achieve. — Optimum Thinking

DEC 2

Daily Gratitude and Intention

Today I am grateful for:
- Balance perception of service to self = service to others
- Look in all areas of life

Today's Flip It:
- Balance perceived negative action/inaction until benefits = drawbacks
- Balance perceived positive action/inaction until drawbacks = benefits

My highest priority actions for tomorrow:

DEC 3

No matter what we talk about, we are talking about ourselves.
— Anonymous

Daily Gratitude and Intention

Today I am grateful for:
- Balance perception of service to self = service to others
- Look in all areas of life

Today's Flip It:
- Balance perceived negative action/inaction until benefits = drawbacks
- Balance perceived positive action/inaction until drawbacks = benefits

My highest priority actions for tomorrow:

Those who have the ability to express gratitude, have far more potential to reach greatness.
— *Optimum Thinking*

DEC 4

Daily Gratitude and Intention

Today I am grateful for:
- Balance perception of service to self = service to others
- Look in all areas of life

Today's Flip It:
- Balance perceived negative action/inaction until benefits = drawbacks
- Balance perceived positive action/inaction until drawbacks = benefits

My highest priority actions for tomorrow:

DEC 5

To believe your own thought, to believe that what is true for you in your private heart is true for all men — that is genius.
— Ralph Waldo Emerson

Daily Gratitude and Intention

Today I am grateful for:
- Balance perception of service to self = service to others
- Look in all areas of life

Today's Flip It:
- Balance perceived negative action/inaction until benefits = drawbacks
- Balance perceived positive action/inaction until drawbacks = benefits

My highest priority actions for tomorrow:

When you feel angry about something someone did to you, ask yourself how what they did will help you achieve what is important to you until you perceive the benefits are equal to the drawbacks. — **Optimum Thinking**

DEC 6

Daily Gratitude and Intention

Today I am grateful for:
- Balance perception of service to self = service to others
- Look in all areas of life

Today's Flip It:
- Balance perceived negative action/inaction until benefits = drawbacks
- Balance perceived positive action/inaction until drawbacks = benefits

My highest priority actions for tomorrow:

DEC 7

If we could understand the order of the universe well enough, we would find that it surpasses all the wishes of the wisest, and that it's impossible to make it better than it is. — Leibniz

Daily Gratitude and Intention

Today I am grateful for:
- Balance perception of service to self = service to others
- Look in all areas of life

Today's Flip It:
- Balance perceived negative action/inaction until benefits = drawbacks
- Balance perceived positive action/inaction until drawbacks = benefits

My highest priority actions for tomorrow:

The most powerful state of attraction is gratitude. — Optimum Thinking

DEC 8

Daily Gratitude and Intention

Today I am grateful for:
- Balance perception of service to self = service to others
- Look in all areas of life

Today's Flip It:
- Balance perceived negative action/inaction until benefits = drawbacks
- Balance perceived positive action/inaction until drawbacks = benefits

My highest priority actions for tomorrow:

DEC 9

Find a job you love and you add five days to every week.
— H. Jackson Brown Jr

Daily Gratitude and Intention

Today I am grateful for:
- Balance perception of service to self = service to others
- Look in all areas of life

Today's Flip It:
- Balance perceived negative action/inaction until benefits = drawbacks
- Balance perceived positive action/inaction until drawbacks = benefits

My highest priority actions for tomorrow:

You are the only person who can inspire you — it is a feeling in your heart. You are in control of your emotional state. What emotional state do you want to create today? — **Optimum Thinking**

DEC 10

Daily Gratitude and Intention

Today I am grateful for:
- Balance perception of service to self = service to others
- Look in all areas of life

Today's Flip It:
- Balance perceived negative action/inaction until benefits = drawbacks
- Balance perceived positive action/inaction until drawbacks = benefits

My highest priority actions for tomorrow:

DEC 11

Minds are like parachutes; they work best when open.
— Lord Thomas Dewar

Daily Gratitude and Intention

Today I am grateful for:
- Balance perception of service to self = service to others
- Look in all areas of life

Today's Flip It:
- Balance perceived negative action/inaction until benefits = drawbacks
- Balance perceived positive action/inaction until drawbacks = benefits

My highest priority actions for tomorrow:

When you feel guilty about something you did to someone, ask yourself how what you did helped them achieve what is important to them until you perceive the benefits to them are equal to the drawbacks. — *Optimum Thinking*

DEC 12

Daily Gratitude and Intention

Today I am grateful for:
- Balance perception of service to self = service to others
- Look in all areas of life

Today's Flip It:
- Balance perceived negative action/inaction until benefits = drawbacks
- Balance perceived positive action/inaction until drawbacks = benefits

My highest priority actions for tomorrow:

DEC 13

Of all the attitudes we can acquire, surely the attitude of gratitude is the most important and by far the most life-changing. — Zig Ziglar

Daily Gratitude and Intention

Today I am grateful for:
- Balance perception of service to self = service to others
- Look in all areas of life

Today's Flip It:
- Balance perceived negative action/inaction until benefits = drawbacks
- Balance perceived positive action/inaction until drawbacks = benefits

My highest priority actions for tomorrow:

DEC 14

Optimum Thinking ... when positive thinking just isn't enough. — Optimum Thinking

Daily Gratitude and Intention

Today I am grateful for:
- Balance perception of service to self = service to others
- Look in all areas of life

Today's Flip It:
- Balance perceived negative action/inaction until benefits = drawbacks
- Balance perceived positive action/inaction until drawbacks = benefits

My highest priority actions for tomorrow:

DEC 15

Life is under no obligation to give us what we expect.
— Margaret Mitchell

Daily Gratitude and Intention

Today I am grateful for:
- Balance perception of service to self = service to others
- Look in all areas of life

Today's Flip It:
- Balance perceived negative action/inaction until benefits = drawbacks
- Balance perceived positive action/inaction until drawbacks = benefits

My highest priority actions for tomorrow:

You will only be able to express true gratitude when you fully appreciate your efforts and how people's challenge and support has helped you achieve what is important to you. — Optimum Thinking

DEC 16

Daily Gratitude and Intention

Today I am grateful for:
- Balance perception of service to self = service to others
- Look in all areas of life

Today's Flip It:
- Balance perceived negative action/inaction until benefits = drawbacks
- Balance perceived positive action/inaction until drawbacks = benefits

My highest priority actions for tomorrow:

DEC 17

I am open to the guidance of synchronicity, and do not let expectations hinder my path.
— Dalai Lama

Daily Gratitude and Intention

Today I am grateful for:
- Balance perception of service to self = service to others
- Look in all areas of life

Today's Flip It:
- Balance perceived negative action/inaction until benefits = drawbacks
- Balance perceived positive action/inaction until drawbacks = benefits

My highest priority actions for tomorrow:

You have programmed yourself with your beliefs. Bring to mind as many as you can and check if they empower or disempower you. — Optimum Thinking

DEC 18

Daily Gratitude and Intention

Today I am grateful for:
- Balance perception of service to self = service to others
- Look in all areas of life

Today's Flip It:
- Balance perceived negative action/inaction until benefits = drawbacks
- Balance perceived positive action/inaction until drawbacks = benefits

My highest priority actions for tomorrow:

DEC 19

Challenges are what makes life interesting; overcoming them is what makes life meaningful.
— Joshua J. Marine

Daily Gratitude and Intention

Today I am grateful for:
- Balance perception of service to self = service to others
- Look in all areas of life

Today's Flip It:
- Balance perceived negative action/inaction until benefits = drawbacks
- Balance perceived positive action/inaction until drawbacks = benefits

My highest priority actions for tomorrow:

You change disempowering beliefs by finding new data that supports a more empowering belief until you choose to adopt it. — Optimum Thinking

DEC 20

Daily Gratitude and Intention

Today I am grateful for:
- Balance perception of service to self = service to others
- Look in all areas of life

Today's Flip It:
- Balance perceived negative action/inaction until benefits = drawbacks
- Balance perceived positive action/inaction until drawbacks = benefits

My highest priority actions for tomorrow:

DEC 21

Reality doesn't bite, rather our perception of reality bites.
— Anthony J. D'Angelo

Daily Gratitude and Intention

Today I am grateful for:
- Balance perception of service to self = service to others
- Look in all areas of life

Today's Flip It:
- Balance perceived negative action/inaction until benefits = drawbacks
- Balance perceived positive action/inaction until drawbacks = benefits

My highest priority actions for tomorrow:

Observe groups who are operating in a highly productive manner and notice how they are supporting and challenging each other to achieve what they want. You will become more aware of what creates conflict in future situations. — Optimum Thinking

DEC 22

Daily Gratitude and Intention

Today I am grateful for:
- Balance perception of service to self = service to others
- Look in all areas of life

Today's Flip It:
- Balance perceived negative action/inaction until benefits = drawbacks
- Balance perceived positive action/inaction until drawbacks = benefits

My highest priority actions for tomorrow:

DEC 23

Our bodies are our gardens — our wills are our gardeners. — William Shakespeare

Daily Gratitude and Intention

Today I am grateful for:
- Balance perception of service to self = service to others
- Look in all areas of life

Today's Flip It:
- Balance perceived negative action/inaction until benefits = drawbacks
- Balance perceived positive action/inaction until drawbacks = benefits

My highest priority actions for tomorrow:

Be grateful for your negative thinking; it is designed to help you work out what you DON'T want. — Optimum Thinking

DEC 24

Daily Gratitude and Intention

Today I am grateful for:
- Balance perception of service to self = service to others
- Look in all areas of life

Today's Flip It:
- Balance perceived negative action/inaction until benefits = drawbacks
- Balance perceived positive action/inaction until drawbacks = benefits

My highest priority actions for tomorrow:

DEC 25

The only real mistake is the one from which we learn nothing. — John Powell

Daily Gratitude and Intention

Today I am grateful for:
- Balance perception of service to self = service to others
- Look in all areas of life

Today's Flip It:
- Balance perceived negative action/inaction until benefits = drawbacks
- Balance perceived positive action/inaction until drawbacks = benefits

My highest priority actions for tomorrow:

> If, at the end of a day you are feeling really proud enjoy it for a moment and then ask yourself who you could have served better today to bring yourself back to being equal to others (Optimum Dog) before you attract external humbling circumstances to do it for you.
> — Optimum Thinking

DEC 26

Daily Gratitude and Intention

Today I am grateful for:
- Balance perception of service to self = service to others
- Look in all areas of life

Today's Flip It:
- Balance perceived negative action/inaction until benefits = drawbacks
- Balance perceived positive action/inaction until drawbacks = benefits

My highest priority actions for tomorrow:

DEC 27

It is one of the most beautiful compensations of this life that no man can sincerely try to help another without helping himself. — Ralph Waldo Emerson

Daily Gratitude and Intention

Today I am grateful for:
- Balance perception of service to self = service to others
- Look in all areas of life

....
....
....
....
....
....
....
....
....
....
....
....

Today's Flip It:
- Balance perceived negative action/inaction until benefits = drawbacks
- Balance perceived positive action/inaction until drawbacks = benefits

....
....
....
....
....

My highest priority actions for tomorrow:
....
....
....
....

When you feel a strong negative emotional charge, first ask yourself what unrealistic expectations you may have in that moment. — Optimum Thinking

DEC 28

Daily Gratitude and Intention

Today I am grateful for:
- Balance perception of service to self = service to others
- Look in all areas of life

Today's Flip It:
- Balance perceived negative action/inaction until benefits = drawbacks
- Balance perceived positive action/inaction until drawbacks = benefits

My highest priority actions for tomorrow:

DEC 29

Learning the game of power requires a certain way of looking at the world, a shifting of perspective.
— Robert Greene

Daily Gratitude and Intention

Today I am grateful for:
- Balance perception of service to self = service to others
- Look in all areas of life

....
....
....
....
....
....
....
....
....
....
....
....

Today's Flip It:
- Balance perceived negative action/inaction until benefits = drawbacks
- Balance perceived positive action/inaction until drawbacks = benefits

....
....
....
....
....
....

My highest priority actions for tomorrow:

....
....
....
....

If you want to create and sustain connected meaningful relationships, make sure you understand each other's goals so you can support their achievement and they can support yours. — Optimum Thinking

DEC 30

Daily Gratitude and Intention

Today I am grateful for:
- Balance perception of service to self = service to others
- Look in all areas of life

Today's Flip It:
- Balance perceived negative action/inaction until benefits = drawbacks
- Balance perceived positive action/inaction until drawbacks = benefits

My highest priority actions for tomorrow:

DEC 31

We do not see things as they are; we see things as we are. — The Talmud

Daily Gratitude and Intention

Today I am grateful for:
- Balance perception of service to self = service to others
- Look in all areas of life

Today's Flip It:
- Balance perceived negative action/inaction until benefits = drawbacks
- Balance perceived positive action/inaction until drawbacks = benefits

My highest priority actions for tomorrow:

A Work in Progress

Life is a work in progress and so is this journal. Please contact us if you have any suggestions as to how to improve it or quotes you think should be added in the next edition. Simply email info@OptimumThinking.net

You can also join our mailing list by filling in the eNews form on our homepage www.OptimumThinking.net.

We look forward to receiving your feedback and suggestions.

www.ingramcontent.com/pod-product-compliance
Lightning Source LLC
Chambersburg PA
CBHW080858010526
44118CB00015B/2185